LINCOLN CHRISTIAN COLLEGE

P9-CQM-189

Breaking the
Language Barrier

Breaking the Language Barrier

Creating Your Own Pathway to Success

H. Douglas Brown

With a Foreword by
Senator Paul Simon

INTERCULTURAL PRESS, INC.

For information contact:
Intercultural Press, Inc.
P.O. Box 700
Yarmouth, ME 04096

Copyright © 1991 by H. Douglas Brown
All rights reserved. No part of this publication may be reproduced in any
manner whatsoever without written permission from the publisher, except in
the case of brief quotations embodied in critical articles or reviews.

Cover design by LetterSpace.
Book design by Jacques Chazaud.

Printed in the United States of America.
95 94 93 92   5 4 3 2 1

Library of Congress Cataloging-in-Publication data

Brown, H. Douglas. 1941-
    Breaking the language barrier: creating your own pathway to
success/H. Douglas Brown: with a foreword by Senator Paul Simon.
        p.   cm.
    Includes bibliographical references and index.
    ISBN 0-933662-91-2
    1. Language and languages—Study and teaching. I. Title.
P51.B76   1991
418'.007—dc20   90-29038
                                                              CIP

Dedication

To my parents, Harry and Ethel Brown,
for giving me a multilingual childhood.

86769

Dedication

CONTENTS

Many people have experienced frustration and failure
trying to learn a foreign language. Languages are important
for building international awareness. What is involved in
learning a foreign language? Successful learning is possible
if you understand the process and create your own preferred
pathway to proficiency.

How do little children learn to talk in the first place? What
can a foreign language learner gain from those insights?

PREFACE

For several decades now, foreign languages have been taught in public schools and universities in the United States with the ostensible goal of producing learners who can actually communicate in the foreign language, that is, who can speak the language with some facility and also understand the language. But our educational goals have gone awry. Of those who have engaged in this classroom struggle for language mastery, only a few have been able to claim that the classroom really led to communicative fluency in a language. What went wrong? Why didn't we learn to communicate?

Breaking the Language Barrier is an answer to those questions. Recent research on foreign language learning has rather suddenly revealed a great deal about what has gone wrong with our language classes. That same research tells us something about what language learners can do to become successful in their efforts. By drawing on current knowledge about the process of foreign language learning, this book sheds some light on how people can take creative, positive steps to improve their chances of success. It does not attempt to tell a teacher how to teach a language—though teachers could derive benefits for their classrooms. The book is aimed at learners who are about to study a foreign language or are presently in a foreign language class. Readers are given specific principles of learning that will help them to become fluent, perhaps in spite of the teaching methods being used.

The book may also speak to those who struggled through foreign language classes only to come out in the end with a few vocabulary items, some stock phrases—"Hello, how are you? I'm fine, thanks. How much does this cost? Goodbye"—and a pronounced distaste for foreign languages.

What we need most in this time of global awareness is an appreciation for languages, a facility for them, and an exorcism of the fear that grows within us as we mispronounce, misunderstand, and misread just about everything imaginable. Current research tells us that those fears can be overcome and that if we give ourselves the right kind of opportunities, we can learn foreign languages successfully.

Breaking the Language Barrier conveys those research findings in a simple, straightforward fashion. There is no mysterious jargon, no lofty academic prose, just plain talk—without compromising the complexity of research in the field—about a phenomenon that is familiar to many. As readers begin to comprehend the factors that make up the process of foreign language learning, they are led to see how they might transform themselves into good language learners through a number of practical steps.

The last chapter deals with creating one's own pathway to success. First, a series of self-tests are introduced and interpreted. The tests are designed to reveal relevant cognitive styles and personality traits that affect the foreign language learning process. Then, a twelve-step program for better language learning is presented. This individualized program is best followed while the learner is engaged in a foreign language course of instruction. By carefully attending to the program, users should be able to put into practice many of the insights and principles offered in the previous nine chapters.

I bring to this book a varied set of experiences in learning foreign languages. I grew up in Zaire, formerly the Belgian Congo, speaking English and Lontomba and subsequently learned Lingala, Kikongo, and

Tshiluba. During my school years, I spent a year in a Belgian school and learned French, along with some Dutch (Flemish), which was a required part of the first-grade curriculum. Later, in high school, I took classroom Latin and French. In college I studied more French and added classroom German. In graduate school I studied a little Hebrew and Greek and struggled through one disastrous semester of Tagalog. Since then, in various international travels, I have picked up some survival phrases in Spanish, Italian, Japanese, Serbo-Croatian, Greek, and Arabic. I have had both successes and failures on this rocky road. Reaping the benefits of natural language learning as a child, I learned to cope with the difficulties of classroom learning and to endure the embarrassments of making my way through strange countries with a bare minimum of language at my command. Those learning experiences, coupled with my twenty years of teaching and research on second language acquisition, form the background for this book.

I am grateful to a number of people who have assisted me in bringing this book to its final form. Kathleen Bailey was especially helpful since she provided constructively critical insights directed at keeping me honest with research findings in the field. Susan Checkley gave invaluable assistance as she meticulously applied her perceptive editorial pen to the final draft of the manuscript. Language learners Rick and Sandy Mitchell and Anita Stockton offered candid reactions from outside the professional field. My college-student daughter, Stefanie, and wife, Mary (both of them classroom language learners), were delightfully tough-minded in their criticisms. Kathy Davis, Elizabeth Leite, and Sandra McKay also provided useful comments. And I am, as always, deeply appreciative of all my graduate students who, through the years, have been a great source of wisdom and inspiration.

Foreword

The world grows smaller every day, and now, more than ever, Americans need foreign language fluency. As I wrote in the introduction to my 1980 book, *The Tongue-Tied American: Confronting the Foreign Language Crisis,* "cultural isolation is a luxury the United States can no longer afford." For American diplomats, scientists, and businessmen to operate effectively internationally and gain access to other cultures, they must be able to speak foreign languages with fluency. But despite recent, scattered improvements in raising the foreign language requirement at the high school and university levels, the United States still lags far behind other nations in exposing students and citizens to learning programs leading to a working fluency in any foreign language.

Part of the problem, of course, is the need to devote more resources to this area. With the marked decline of federal funding for the study of foreign languages and cultures in the 1970s, both undergraduate enrollments and serious scholarship suffered. Private foundations have to some extent continued support for such study, but they rightly expect government at all levels to sustain these programs. Fortunately, a renewed debate in recent years about American education and the role it plays in our international economic competitiveness has begun to create the political will to renew our lagging commitment to foreign language training.

Another part of the problem, however, is what most Americans view as the intimidating nature of foreign language study. Many Americans—students as well as those beyond school and university years—find it difficult to get started or to retain what they have been taught. Dr. Brown's important book provides timely help with this problem. It does so by demystifying the language learning process, explaining how we learn and remember, and assisting the reader to map out a successful study program of his or her own. It is a much needed guide for all of us nonspecialists who are interested in learning a foreign language.

This book should increase the success rate for readers who use it in studying foreign languages and help them enjoy themselves while they are learning.

Senator Paul Simon
Washington, D.C.

Acknowledgments

Some of the examples and anecdotes in this book also appear in *A Practical Guide to Language Learning*, by H. Douglas Brown. New York: McGraw Hill, Inc., 1989.

Grateful acknowledgment is made to the following for permission to reprint copyrighted material.

United Media: *Peanuts* cartoons (Figs. 4, 9, 11); *Frank 'n Ernest* cartoons (Figs. 3, 10); *Born Loser* cartoons (Figs. 2, 13); *Drabble* cartoon (Fig. 6).

King Features Syndicate: *Krazy Kat* cartoon (Fig. 1); *Family Circus* cartoon (Fig. 5).

Creators Syndicate: *B.C.* cartoon (Fig. 14).

Rick Horowitz: "Politics to the Max," copyright 1986.

Lawrence Erlbaum Associates, Inc.: Robert W. Norton, "Measurement of Ambiguity Tolerance," *Journal of Personality Assessment*, 39, copyright 1975.

Scholastic Testing Service, Inc.: E. Paul Torrance, "Your Style of Learning and Thinking," copyright 1987.

The Psychological Corporation: "Pimsleur Language Aptitude Battery."

BREAKING THE
LANGUAGE BARRIER

1

Can I Learn
a Foreign Language?

You don't have to look very far these days to find an advertisement that reads something like this: "Learn a foreign language fast! At home or in your car. $14.95," or "What would you give to learn a foreign language? Try $125." The advertisements promise phenomenal—and almost instant—success if you'll only follow a programmed set of cassette tapes, sometimes sold with a tape recorder or even a "handsome attaché case." By the end of the program, you will have taught yourself to "speak like a diplomat" in the foreign language! (They neglect to note that American diplomats aren't known the world over as paragons of fluency in foreign languages.)

With materials like these around, you have to wonder why everyone in the United States isn't bilingual by now. We are led to believe that these do-it-yourself language courses will teach us a foreign language painlessly. How is it that 250 million people have missed this opportunity? Do-it-yourself-minded America wouldn't pass up the chance to learn something so complex and so useful if we could so easily fulfill the prophecy of the advertisers.

Those millions of you who struggled through foreign language classes in high school or college can take heart. You haven't missed out on some well-kept secret. Your bitter struggle with those infernal grammar rules, monotonous drills, and bizarre little dialogues could not have been replaced by a cheap set of instant recipes for success. Your classes could well have been enhanced by some of these programs, but home-study cassette programs, in and of themselves, will rarely if ever produce a proficient speaker of a foreign language. A well-designed and effectively taught course in a foreign language gives you a far better chance of success. Even those courses, though, depend on your own intrinsic motivation and just plain hard work for ultimate success. Don't let anyone fool you into believing that success in learning a foreign language comes about effortlessly.

Tongue-tied Americans

What's gone wrong with foreign language instruction? A casual glance at results of foreign language teaching in our schools and universities reveals some depressing statistics. Those classes aren't doing the job either. Americans are inexcusably monolingual. We're victims of what Senator William Fulbright[1] called "linguistic and cultural myopia." In *The Tongue-Tied American*, Senator Paul Simon[2] said America was "linguistically malnourished." We have assumed that our language is universal; after all, you can go virtually anywhere in the world now and find someone who speaks English. Why, then, should Americans even bother to learn a foreign language?

By the late seventies that motivation was so low that President Carter appointed the twenty-five-member President's Commission on Foreign Language and International Studies to study the situation. The commission's report[3] described the "scandalous incompetence" of Americans in foreign languages. Among their findings:

- Only about half of the high school students who took the first year of a foreign language went on to a second year, and fewer than 4 percent of all high school students went on to a third. (In many other countries, secondary school students must take at least four years of a foreign language.)

- One-half million fewer U.S. high school students were enrolled in foreign language classes in 1974 than in 1968, despite a growth in total student enrollment.
- In 1966 about 34 percent of U.S. colleges required foreign language study for admission, compared to only 8 percent in 1979.
- Fifty-four percent fewer college students enrolled in foreign language courses in 1974 than in 1963, despite a rapidly rising U.S. dependence on exports.
- There were at least 10,000 English-speaking Japanese business representatives in the U.S. but fewer than 900 Japanese-speaking American business representatives in Japan.
- Foreign language teaching at the elementary school level had virtually disappeared, reaching less than 1 percent of all students.

Figure 1

In an era when global interdependence is growing by leaps and bounds, we seem to be strangely insular. The Soviet Union has more teachers of English than the United States has students of Russian. A few years ago the Japanese trade minister announced that Nippon Telephone and Telegraph had ninety million dollars to lend at very low interest rates to foreign investors, but not one American company applied because the application had to be written in Japanese. When Pepsi-Cola makers started to advertise in Thailand, they used the American slogan, "Come alive, you're in the Pepsi generation." Only later did the company realize that the slogan was mistakenly translated as, "Pepsi brings your ancestors back from the dead."

Meanwhile, immigrants continue to pour into this country demanding English instruction. Foreign students come to the U.S. and learn English in order to enter our universities. English as a second language (ESL) has become a household term as we inch toward one billion speakers of English (with more than half speaking English as their second language) across the globe. Americans haven't followed suit. In some cases, we've gone in the opposite direction. Certain political action groups, in a misguided fear that the increasing number of speakers of other languages in our country will somehow "diminish" the English language, have begun to push for "English-only" legislation to "protect" our language.

But there are signs of hope as some of the recommendations of the Carter Commission are now being implemented. Enrollments in foreign language classes have increased moderately in the last five years—dramatically so in Chinese, Japanese, and Russian. Some colleges and universities have reinstated their abandoned foreign language requirements. Lobby groups like the Joint National Committee for Languages are stressing legislation that favors funding of bilingual and foreign language instruction. Even an Association to Cure Monolingualism has been founded to promote language teaching in the schools. And, most importantly, teachers are now getting better professional training, and methods and materials for teaching foreign languages are improving significantly.

Some other encouraging facts:

- The U.S. government employs over thirty thousand persons a year with a working knowledge of foreign languages.
- The State Department considers foreign language skills as highly desirable for senior promotions.
- Many U.S. airlines favor applicants who have foreign language skills.

- Over 850 radio stations in the U.S. broadcast in fifty-eight foreign languages.
- About half of all U.S. multinational company executives know foreign languages.
- The Chase Manhattan Bank does more recruiting at the Georgetown Center for Strategic and International Studies than it does at Harvard Business School.
- A survey of 1,200 companies in the U.S. reported over sixty thousand positions requiring employees with a knowledge of a second language.
- Major U.S. companies routinely employ from five hundred to five thousand persons in other countries.[4]

Becoming a successful language learner

You are probably reading this book because you are about to, or have recently started to, learn a foreign language yourself. You want to know how you can succeed in your endeavor. The bad news is that the task ahead of you is difficult and even grueling. You won't succeed through any sort of painless, neatly packaged program of cassette tapes. And there is no teaching method out there that is foolproof. Nor can you be guaranteed success if you study under the world's best language teacher.

The good news is that you *can*, by taking control of your own learning, be a successful language learner. We now know a great deal about the language learning process, and the research findings keep coming in. That research tells us that virtually everyone has abilities, resources, and experiences that they can tap into. By understanding your own strengths and abilities, you can develop pathways to success. Those pathways may turn out to be a unique network of intellectual and emotional routes—unlike those of any other learner. No single formula works equally well for all people.

The remaining chapters of this book are designed to help you build those individualized pathways to success. As you increasingly understand the factors that are involved in this most complex of human learning experiences, you'll be able to derive principles for your own learning process. Those principles will form a sort of "battle plan" for "attacking" the foreign language. You will come to recognize the pitfalls that can so easily entrap you, and you'll learn how to avoid them. You will be able to identify the benchmarks of success and figure out how to capitalize on them. Best of all, you'll understand yourself better as a thinking, feeling, and acting person and can then channel that understanding into a sense of private ownership of your own successful techniques for internalizing the foreign language.

If you happen to be a reader who was at one time (but who is no longer) a student of a foreign language, and especially if you were among the 90 percent who were rather *un*successful in the quest for language proficiency, you might be curious about why you fell short of achieving fluency in the language. Most of us considered ourselves lucky just to preserve our sanity throughout the wearisome process of memorizing vocabulary, reciting idiotic sentences in class, and translating rather simple-minded passages about the importance of the Rhine River. Some of us who were fortunate enough to travel to the country of our dreams were shocked and bewildered to discover upon arrival that we could scarcely understand a single word being uttered by those around us. What went wrong? Why didn't we learn to communicate?

For those of you who happen to be foreign language teachers, some of the ideas in this book could start your creative juices flowing so that your classes will untie the tongues of your students. Too many of us were left with a strong distaste for foreign languages after we struggled through them at school, and innovative teaching methods could be a key to converting what might otherwise be failures into successes.

The bottom line here is that, as a language learner, you can—and must—take control of your own language learning and assume responsibility for your success or failure. This book should speed you on your way.

2

How Babies
Learn to Talk

They heared 'em underground cau-cause they went through a hoyle—a hole—and they pulled a rock from underground and then they saw a wave going in—that the hole—and they brought a table and the wave brought 'em out the k-tunnel and then the—they went away and then—uh—m—ah—back on top and it was—uh—going under a bridge and they went—then the braves hit the—the bridge—they—all of it—th-then they looked there—then they—then they were safe.

No, there's nothing wrong with this child's language ability. As you try to make some sense out of it, you may be tempted to wonder what sort of speech therapy she requires. But what you have read here is a verbatim transcription of a normal five-year-old girl's retelling of a story she has just seen on TV. The surprising thing is not so much her "mistakes," but that when we actually hear a child speaking, we are quite capable of ignoring the backtracking, hesitations, repetitions, and undecipherable phrases and words, in favor of grasping the overall meaning the child is trying to convey. Those of us who listen to young children hear this sort of language all the time and think nothing of it.

But then an excerpt like this also reminds us that children are learning a tremendously complex skill when they learn their mother tongue. Learning to talk—which every so-called normal child does with natural ease—is tricky business.

Baby talk—a tall order

We have all witnessed the remarkable ability of children to communicate. Small babies babble and coo and cry and send an extraordinary number of vocal and nonvocal messages daily. They receive even more. Around the one-year mark they make specific attempts to imitate words and speech sounds they hear around them and their first recognizable words appear. By about eighteen months these words have multiplied considerably and begin to appear in combination with each other in two- or three-word *telegraphic* utterances like "allgone milk," "bye-bye Daddy," and "Mommy give cookie." The production tempo now begins to increase as more and more words and combinations of two-, three-, and four-word "sentences" emerge. By about age three, children's speech capacity has mushroomed—they generate nonstop chatter, and their linguistic genius becomes a mixed blessing to those around them. Their fluency continues to grow, and by school age, children not only know what to say but what *not* to say, as they also learn the social nature of language.

How can we explain this fantastic journey from that first cry at birth to adult competence in a native language? from one word to tens of thousands? from telegraphese at eighteen months to compound-complex, precise, socially appropriate sentences just a few short years later? What, after all, do we mean by the word *language*? And then, what is involved in learning a language?

Sounds. When you learn your mother tongue, you learn dozens of individual sounds and a system of sound combinations. You learn how to manipulate your lips, tongue, cheeks, and throat in such precise ways that you can produce a particular set of sounds (out of the universe of possibilities) that is recognizable as English. You learn how to connect those sounds together and how to make subtle changes in an individual sound to fit the sound that is next to it. For example, you learn to say, "ju-eet?" which is easily understood as "Did you eat?" or "I-o-wanna," meaning "I don't want to." You learn how to "sing" the appropriate intonation patterns of sounds to convey questions, emphasis, and many different emotions. You learn the system of *stressing* certain syllables, of placing pauses and stops between words, word groups, and sentences. You learn the effect of rhythm, speed, volume, and pitch. All this, just for the sound system of a language.

Words. By the time young people finish high school, they know somewhere between 100,000 and 200,000 words.[5] A little mathematics will tell you that is an average of about 5,500 to 11,000 words a year—or between fifteen and thirty words a day. And that doesn't allow for words you learned and then forgot—or for weekends, or holidays, or sick days. Can you actually imagine learning up to thirty words a day for the first eighteen years of your life? When did you learn those words? In school? Hardly. Who taught you? Teachers? Maybe some of the words, but the overwhelming number of them were just absorbed. You heard them, you read them, then perhaps you used them when you talked or wrote something, and then they were just "there."

Grammar. All children learn a very complex grammatical system in the native language, whether they like it or not. I'm not talking about the grammar that teachers tell us about when we learn that "a noun is the name of a person, place, or thing." I'm talking about the system of rules that we all subconsciously internalize that tells us way down deep somewhere how to string all these sounds and words together in such a way that others will understand us. Grammar is what tells us that a sentence like "Bill air kite the blue a saw in" is undecipherable in that word order, but that a sentence like "Bill saw a blue kite in the air" is okay. Grammar also tells us that sentences like "Colorless green ideas sleep furiously" and "'Twas brillig and the slithy toves, did gyre and gimble in the wabe" are probably okay grammatically; it's just the words that are confusing. Children manage to learn everything from very simple word order to quite complex sentence structure without ever having to pass a language arts class.

Pragmatics. Yet another staggeringly complex aspect of language that you learned as a child is called *pragmatics*. That is, you didn't just learn sounds, words, rules for making sentences, and rules for stringing sentences together. You also learned how language is based on context. You learned that if someone says "Do you know what time it is?" your answer, if you have a watch on, should not be a simple yes. Your pragmatic knowledge tells you that the following exchange is perfectly understandable:

[phone rings, child picks up phone]
JANE:	Hello...
VOICE ON PHONE:	Hi, Jane, is your mom there?
JANE:	Just a minute. [yells] Mom! Phone!
MOM:	[from another room] I'm in the tub!
JANE:	[to the person on the phone] She can't come now. May I take a message?

Jane understands that (a) the person on the phone wants to speak to her mother and that (b) her mother is unable to come and speak on the phone, both without any *direct* communication of those facts. Because of her awareness of the context of the communication, Jane was able to use her pragmatic knowledge of language to decipher (and to convey) information.

Pragmatics also includes a whole host of competencies that enable us to behave politely and appropriately in our culture. Children learn how to use language for their own ends. And their language extends even beyond words to all of the nonverbal signals (gestures, facial expression, eye contact, touching, distance between speakers, etc.) that sometimes contain more information than verbal language.

Innate capacities

Linguists sometimes explain how children can absorb so much information by arguing that a fair amount of children's linguistic capacity is innate. That is, human beings are born with a set of genes or brain cells that enable them to take in all this complex information in a very short time.

Now, don't misunderstand the concept of innateness. It doesn't mean that a child is born with a predisposition toward a particular language. Legend has it that the ancient Egyptian king Psammeticus once set out to discover the "true" language of the human race. To do so he conducted an experiment. He isolated a newborn infant in a small room in his palace for many months and supposedly prevented the child from hearing human voices until it had uttered its first word. When that occurred, the word was—you guessed it—Egyptian. Psammeticus concluded, of course, that Egyptian was the true and universal language. Unfortunately, Psammeticus neglected to control his experiment by replicating it in Babylonia, China, or other kingdoms.

Figure 2

The child's capacity for language acquisition is thought to be inborn because children don't have enough minutes and hours in their short lives to "learn" everything involved in the process. The noted MIT linguist Noam Chomsky[6] and his followers claimed that all human beings (as opposed to animals) are born with what they termed a "language acquisition device" or "LAD." The LAD isn't really a device.

It's not a "little black box" that occupies a certain cerebral territory. It's a set of genetically transmitted capacities that all children are born with, enabling the human brain to distinguish speech sounds from other sounds in the environment, to search for certain universal properties of language (words, pauses between words, word order significance, classes of words, symbolic reference, etc.), and to persist in the imitation of speech as it gets increasingly complex. These are universal properties that apply to whichever actual language the child is exposed to.

The LAD doesn't operate only in the first couple of years of life, according to the experts. One linguist, Derek Bickerton,[7] noted that the innate properties of the LAD are evident throughout a period of as much as a decade of linguistic development. As a flower seed is *programmed* to produce successive stages of roots, stem, leaves, buds, and blossoms, so the human LAD is *bioprogrammed* to release certain capacities at certain stages. For example, English-speaking children tend, at the age of three or so, to learn to talk about the past with what appear to be correct irregular verb forms: "I wrote...," "She broke...," "They drank...," etc. Then, around the age of four or five, they begin to perceive a system of past tense formation in which an *ed* ending is added to verbs. Quite abruptly they begin to say "I writed...," "She breaked...," and "They drinked...." Have they regressed? No, what has happened is that their bioprogram tells them to systematize, or regularize, past tenses of verbs—all past tenses. Then, a year or two later, that same bioprogram releases the capacity to distinguish between regular verbs (walk/walked, talk/talked, etc.) and irregular verbs (break/broke, drink/drank, etc.).

The implications of the bioprogramming theory are that all children experience a "critical period" for language acquisition between birth and puberty. During this time children must pass through certain developmental stages in order for linguistic development to progress. While some children are faster or slower than others, they all nevertheless go through the stages in sequence. If for some reason—say, a stroke, mental disease, or extreme isolation from other human beings (as in the case of a number of reported "wolf children" who have been reared by animals)—the child misses a major stage, language will be retarded.

Claims for the innateness of language capacity have been criticized by those who insist on scientific proof. Ambrose Bierce provided this wry comment in his hilarious *The Devil's Dictionary*: "The doctrine of innate ideas is one of the most admirable faiths of philosophy, being itself an innate idea and therefore inaccessible to disproof."[8] Nevertheless, evidence from dozens of languages around the world continues to lend support to the concept of the innate properties of language. It seems that no matter what language children acquire as their mother tongue, there are many similar processes governing them all.

With some certainty, then, we can fall back on innateness as a partial explanation for how children manage to master such a complicated skill at a relatively young age. But innateness theories seem quite hypothetical and esoteric when it comes to giving us practical, down-to-earth explanations of what it is a child *does* over those first few years of life to be so successful. Saying that language learning capacity is innate is too pat, too easy a way out. If we dig deeper, we can find more enlightening facets of first-language acquisition—more enlightening, at least, for our understanding of the *process* of development and of the implications of that process for second-language learning. Let's look at some of those other facets.

Language for survival

We acquire language for very direct, meaningful purposes. Language has a "here and now" quality to it that makes it an essential tool to possess. It's the vehicle through which children learn, at a very young age, to manipulate others around them for their own ends. In terms of Maslow's[9] hierarchy of needs, language enables us to satisfy needs for food, drink, warmth, comfort, social stimulation, exploration, knowledge, and ego enhancement. Many centuries ago St. Augustine wrote, in his own wordy, philosophical style, of his motivation for learning language:

> For I was no longer a speechless infant, but a speaking boy. This
> I remember; and have since observed how I learned to speak. It

was not that my elders taught me words...in any set method; but I, longing by cries and broken accents and various motions of my limbs to express my thoughts, that so I might have my will, and yet unable to express all that I willed, or to whom I willed, did myself, by the understanding which Thou, my God, gavest me, practice the sounds in my memory.... And thus by constantly hearing words, as they occurred in various sentences, I collected gradually for what they stood; and having broken in my mouth to these signs, I thereby gave utterance to my will. Thus I exchanged with those about me these current signs of our wills, and so launched deeper into the stormy intercourse of human life.[10]

From the very beginning, children are subconsciously aware of the power of language. Within the first year or so of life, for example, they discover the impact of the word *No!* and use it often—too often, if you poll the mothers and fathers of the world. A few years later they learn the shock value of various taboo words and four-letter expletives. Teenagers seem to run out of conventional modes of expression and engage in their own in-group talk that's like, for sure, totally awesome. Their language has the power of giving them an identity (more on this topic in chapter 7).

Without language we are no longer human. Language defines us; it controls us; and with it we control and define our world. That is why we learn a language: for survival.

Subconscious learning

Children are relatively unaware of the language they use. Up to the age of five or so, they don't think at all about the rules that govern language. They will, of course, ask questions about what words mean ("Dad, what does *respect* mean?"), or they will ask for clarification ("huh?"), but they are not interested in language as a system. They simply want to get at meaning. They don't have the least bit of interest in grammar or correctness. A researcher[11] once asked three-year-old Adam, "Now, Adam, listen to what I say. Tell me which is better to say...*some* water, or...*a* water." Adam nonchalantly replied, "Pop go weasel!" He wanted no part of this senseless inquisition.

Even though children don't think about language, they still have within them rules that tell them that "a water" isn't what people say. A child language researcher named Jean Berko[12] once showed conclusively that children as young as age four have rules that work, even on words that they don't know. Berko found that she could get four-year-olds to demonstrate their subconscious knowledge of rules by giving them nonsense words. For example, a picture of a little blob was given the name *wug*. Then a picture of two blobs was presented to the children and they were told, "Now there are two of them. There are two _____." Children at this age easily supplied the grammatically correct *wugs*. Similarly, these same children talked about other pictures: people who *gling* every day *glinged* yesterday (a few thought they *glang*), and are now *glinging*, and so forth. The system is in place, and it's alive and well; it's merely beneath consciousness.

"That's not how you say it!"

The child's subconscious stages of acquisition are quite resistant to correction by others unless that correction relates in some way to actual meaning. Consider the following conversation:

CHILD:	Nobody don't like me.
PARENT:	No, say "nobody likes me."
CHILD:	[a little more emphatically] Nobody don't like me.
PARENT:	No, you should say "nobody likes me."
CHILD:	[even more emphatically] *Nobody* don't like me!
PARENT:	No, now listen, carefully. Say "nobody likes me."
CHILD:	Oh! Nobody don't likes me.[13]

The child, of course, only wanted some recognition of her meaningful utterance while the parent wasted time attending to a grammatical point which was, in the child's view, totally irrelevant to the important fact that she feared she was unloved.

A similar incident happened in a first-grade classroom when a teacher asked her pupils to write a few sentences on a piece of paper. One pupil, not finding any pencils in his desk, said, "Teacher, I ain't got no pencil." Disturbed at the fractured English, the teacher embarked on a barrage of corrective models for the child: "I *don't* have *any* pencils, you *don't* have *a* pencil, they don't have pencils...." When the teacher finally ended her monologue of patterns, the intimidated and bewildered child said, "Ain't *nobody* got no pencils?"

This particular child may have been speaking what he perceived as a totally acceptable dialect of English, modeled from adults in his home setting, in which case there was (to him) no "error" at all—all the more reason for him to remain oblivious to the teacher's attempts to draw attention to language patterns. The overall lesson here is that in the case of most young children, we do well to correct their speech only if there is a meaning gap, and then somewhat indirectly. Many of the "errors" take care of themselves—subconsciously—in due course of time.

Creativity

One of the great marvels of the child's first-language acquisition experience is that a skill so complex isn't just being learned in a robot-like, uniform fashion. Rather, every child is uniquely creative. Remember the five-year-old's description of a television show at the beginning of the chapter? Here is another sample of normal five-year-old speech; this time a child is describing part of the *Wizard of Oz* story:

> ...and, and then after that she dreamed—uh—and then she was in her sleep when she woke up and—know what?—she was—she was on her bed but she woke up, and I didn't see her on her bed 'cause was dreaming about she woking up, then she dreamed about her—uh—then—know what?—she saw—[laughing] this is the funny part—[laughing] when the tornado—the tornado blew her mother up she was sewing in a chair [still laughing]! That's the funny part!

Perfectly normal in her speech development, she chose her own way to recreate the story. No other child would have come up with the exact same description of the same story.

A somewhat older child once provided the following written definition of a *bolt* and *nut:*

> A bolt is a thing like a stick of hard metal, such as iron, with a square bunch on one end and a lot of scratching wound around the other end. A nut is similar to the bolt only just the opposite, being a hole in a little chunk of iron sawed off short, with wrinkles inside of the hole.

She knew what a nut and bolt were and described them in a way that was utterly unique.

Children will let language mean anything they, or their hearers, want it to mean. Remember when Lewis Carroll's[14] Alice argued with Humpty Dumpty?

> "There's glory for you!"
> "I don't know what you mean by *glory*," Alice said.
> Humpty Dumpty smiled contemptuously. "Of course you don't—till I tell you. I meant there's 'a nice knock-down argument for you!'"
> "But *glory* doesn't mean 'a nice knock-down argument,'" Alice objected.
> "When *I* use a word," Humpty Dumpty said, in rather a scornful tone, "it means just what I choose it to mean—neither more nor less."
> "The question is," said Alice, "whether you *can* make words mean so many different things."
> "The question is," said Humpty Dumpty, "which is to be master— that's all."

Children, like Humpty Dumpty (Alice is of course being quite the adult here), know how to use language for their own ends. They become masters of the art at a young age. This creativity in language extends through all of our adult life; we continue to create novel sentences almost every time we speak or write.

The importance of comprehension

Sometimes the role of language comprehension is overlooked in observing the first-language development process. We tend to gauge children's linguistic development by what they say. It's clear, however, from extensive research, that comprehension plays a vital role in acquisition and outstrips production (that is, what children say or write). Even as adults we understand more language—more words, more grammatical structures, more rhetorical styles, and more regional or social dialects of a language—than we actually produce orally or in writing. With children, the gap between comprehension and production is sometimes quite obvious. Consider the following conversation:

CHILD:	My name's Litha.
ADULT:	Li*tha*?
CHILD:	No, Litha.
ADULT:	Oh, Li*s*a.
CHILD:	Yeah, that's right, Litha.

Here it's clear that Lisa could hear the difference between a /*th*/ and an /*s*/ sound but couldn't actually say it. At a later point in time, as is the case with virtually all of child language acquisition, Lisa will also be able to say (produce) both sounds.

Figure 3

When you stop to think about it, it's logical to surmise that children will understand more language than they can produce. After all, where do they get language? From others. The input they receive is a crucial factor in language development, and a direct relationship exists between the quality (that is, the variety, the depth, the meaningfulness) of the child's input and the child's total language competence and, ultimately, the child's production capabilities.

The quantity of input—its frequency, repetition, etc.—contrary to what you might intuitively be led to believe, doesn't always bear a strong relationship to output. Some studies[15] in Japan, for example, showed that children produced the Japanese word *ga* (which indicates stronger, more specific emphasis) far more frequently and correctly than another contrasting word *wa* (weaker, more generalized emphasis), even though *wa* occurred twice as often as *ga* in their input. Children don't seem to need a high frequency of certain input in order to learn words or rules in their mother tongue. If a particular unit of language is perceived as being very important (such as the power of a word like *ga* in Japanese), it is easily lodged in the memory. This may help to explain how the human brain can process so much in the relatively short period of child language acquisition.

Still waters may indeed run deep where child language is involved. Children do a great deal of silent, unobservable processing that we adults can't observe. We are certainly unable to judge their language capacities by only listening to what they say.

Language and thought

Does language—or do words in a language—shape thought? Or does thought somehow give rise to language? These are questions that have fascinated linguists and psychologists for many decades. The questions remain only partially answered.

There is no doubt that words shape our lives. The advertising world is a prime example of the use of language to shape, persuade, and dissuade. Advertisers manipulate words and turn quite ordinary items into products that are "unsurpassed," "ultimate," "supercharged," and "the right choice." Food that has been sapped of most of its nutrients by the manufacturing process comes back to us as "enriched" and "fortified." Euphemisms abound in the news media. "Receiving waters" are the lakes into which possibly toxic industrial wastes are dumped. Slums are "substandard dwellings." The development of a system of lethal missiles is referred to as a "peace initiative." "Plausible deniability" means being able to lie. Is there any doubt that language shapes our thinking? Or, at least, that people attempt, through language, to shape thought?

In a rather fascinating experimental study,[16] subjects were presented with a candle, a box of thumbtacks, and two or three matches. Their problem was to attach the candle to a wall in an upright position so that the candle wouldn't drip. One group of subjects was not given any labels; the second group was given four labels: candle, box, tacks, matches. The second group performed the task fifteen times faster than the first group because the first group generally failed to see that the box itself could be a prop in the solution and only saw it as a container for the tacks. What the labels did was focus attention on four separate elements, which led to the perception of the box as the base for the candle. Language influenced thinking.

Children's early conceptual development cannot escape the influence of language. A child sees a dog; someone else says "dog"; the child then says "dog" and is reinforced with smiles. A child sees a horse and says "dog" and is told that it's a "horse." The new label acts as a stimulus to find differences between dogs and horses. Soon thereafter those verbal labels are an important part of the retention of concepts.

Since children are growing intellectually and linguistically at the same time, language interacts with the thinking process to enhance intellectual development. This is, in fact, one of the distinct advantages that children possess over adults. As they rapidly build their conceptual repertoire, their storehouse of language is increasing accordingly. Language aids in retaining and expanding concepts. And concepts help to cement linguistic labels and expression. This interaction extends well beyond puberty as words are used to give labels to thoughts.

Mother-tongue learning

Babies don't learn to talk by magic. Even if some of the capacities are inborn, the process is a complex one that demands time, attention, concentration, and effort. As you move into the next chapter, where you will look at how children learn second languages, you can derive some insights from the first-language acquisition process:

1. Learning one's mother tongue is an incredible accomplishment, but virtually everyone does it.
2. Language itself almost defies complete definition, but just an inkling on your part of the sounds, words, grammar rules, and pragmatic conventions of language is enough to appreciate its complexity.
3. Innate factors may play a large part in enabling the human brain to internalize so much information in a short time.
4. Children are blessed with what appears to be a "critical period" during which they acquire their mother tongue most efficiently; this period may in some way be bioprogrammed.
5. Children use their native language for basic survival, and therefore it becomes as important to them as food, shelter, and other basic needs.
6. Language is internalized subconsciously, without overt conscious processes of thinking about language.
7. Children generate language creatively in ways that are unique and never before rehearsed.
8. Comprehension of the language around them is very important for children; speaking appears to emerge after they have to some extent understood aspects of language.
9. The frequency of input in a child's linguistic surroundings isn't as crucial as the importance a child attaches to linguistic elements.
10. Language helps to shape thinking, and children have the advantage of learning thought and learning language hand in hand, even to the point that thinking can shape language.

3

Whﾶ Children
Cﾶ Teﾶch Us

Five-year-old Jeff sobs in his pillow. Mom and Dad come into his room to console him. "It's okay, Jeff, you'll get used to this new country. In no time flat you'll make new friends, learn the language, and feel right at home." Unmoved, Jeff cries, "Why did we have to move? I hate this place! I can't stand this house. I hate the food. Nobody says anything I can understand in this stupid place. I wanna go back home!"

Mysteriously, one week later Jeff has made some new friends in Egypt. His friends speak Arabic and Jeff thinks they sound sort of funny, but they're nice to him. They are curious about his fair complexion, his fancy toys, and the funny language he speaks. Jeff has decided in this short time that the house is probably okay and that the food isn't all that bad—after all, he couldn't have hot dogs and pizza every day, even back in Illinois.

A month later Jeff is the perfect picture of self-adjustment. The language his friends speak has gotten less and less crazy. In fact, he can be seen daily talking some Arabic himself, using gestures and other nonverbal signals to make himself understood. Every now and then he gives his parents an Arabic word or expression they can't think of themselves, as they struggle with their grueling daily language lessons.

Three months later Jeff is, in his own five-year-old way, fluent. He's a regular chatterbox in Arabic. If he doesn't know something, he simply asks how to say it or gets around the situation nonverbally. He has become self-sufficient in a second language in a matter of three months.

Meanwhile, Mom and Dad struggle. They toil over their Arabic grammar and weekly vocabulary lists; they do their translation exercises daily; whenever possible they try to converse with local colleagues but find the process tiring and discouraging. They observe with wonder the ease with which Jeff has picked up this language and how comfortable he is now in his new surroundings. It is now Jeff who consoles his parents when they express frustration.

"You're not saying it right, Dad. You sound sort of funny when you talk in Arabic. But I guess you'll get it one of these days. It's pretty easy."

We witness scenarios like this one over and over again in the experience of children who are forced to survive in a country where a new language is spoken. They seem to survive with little more than the early discomforts that Jeff felt in the first few days of residence while parents struggle for months and even years with only moderate success in internalizing the new language. What is it that gives the child this marvelous capacity to learn a second* language with such agility? If we knew the secret of the child's success, could we adults recreate the child's capacities within us?

---

* The terms *second* language and *foreign* language are used interchangeably throughout this book. You may run across situations where second-language learning means learning a nonnative language in the country where the language is spoken (say, English in the U.S.A.), and foreign-language learning means learning a nonnative language in a country where that language isn't commonly spoken (say, French in the U.S.A.). Here, rather than trying to make that fine distinction, both terms refer to any language other than the native language, regardless of the context.

First- and second-language learning

Barring extreme abnormalities, every child learns his or her native language to the point of being functional and fluent in it. Learning to talk is as natural as learning to walk. It seems logical, then, that we should emulate those processes that are so successful.

But beware! We are tempted to see a direct analogy between the first-language acquisition of children and the second-language acquisition of adults, when in reality the analogy is quite indirect. An article on tips for second-language learners once incorrectly claimed that "...a small child does not learn formal grammar. You don't tell him about verbs and nouns. Yet he learns the language perfectly. It is equally unnecessary, therefore, for adults to use grammatical conceptualization in learning a foreign language."[17] At first glance, this advice seems to make sense. But further thought should lead you to contemplate the intellectual differences between small children and adults: adults can use abstract thought (about grammar) to their benefit, so why rule it out just because conscious grammatical conceptualization is beyond the capacity of young children?

We have to carefully consider basic intellectual and emotional differences between children and adults before we can draw correct analogies. So, in order to avoid comparing apples and oranges, let's start by briefly comparing first- and second-language learning in children. Then we can go on to look at adult learning processes.

Child second-language learning

Children learn a second language with as much apparent ease as the first. Even in late childhood, the process of second-language learning is highly efficient. That changes in adults.

As we look at child- and adult-learning processes, an operational definition is needed. Puberty is a key point for differentiating between children and adults. From the perspective of intellectual as well as emotional development, the age of twelve or thirteen brings about important changes. As we shall see, puberty also appears to usher in some changes in the way our language-learning processes operate.

With that operational definition in mind, let's look briefly at how children's first- and second-language acquisition processes compare.

Innateness. If human beings are bioprogrammed for first-language development up through puberty, then there is reason to believe that a bioprogram would operate in second-language learning as well.

Critical period. Most research supports a *critical period*—for pronunciation of a second language, at least—that lasts through puberty. That is, children will attain authentic, nativelike accents in the second language. If a second language is begun after puberty, however, there is a high probability of retaining a foreign accent.

Language for survival. Learning a second language can be as much a matter of survival as learning the first. If children are in contexts where they simply must use the second language in order to play, to succeed in school, or to meet their personal needs and wants, their instinct for survival will motivate them.

Subconscious learning. Younger children internalize a second language as subconsciously as their first. As they approach puberty, however, there is more likelihood of intellectualizing the process to the point that they become overly aware of their own learning. If students are taught a foreign language in a classroom where a teacher calls attention to grammar and other language rules, they can easily be induced into an unnatural, premature overawareness.

Creativity. Children are just as creative in the second language as they are in the first.

Importance of comprehension. Here too, there appears to be no difference in the intensity with which children attend to language around them, whether they are in a first- or second-language learning mode. And the importance, not the frequency, of input is the crucial factor.

Language and thought. There are differences between older and younger children in attaching language to thinking and vice versa. Older monolingual children have had a number of years to grow accustomed to a close connection between conceptual development and their first language. A second language begun at age eight or nine, for example, takes on an adjunct relationship to concept development. Sometimes that relationship enhances intellectual development; sometimes it hinders it. There is conflicting research on this issue, an issue that has stirred hot debate on whether or not to provide bilingual education for elementary school children who don't speak English. The significant fact for your consideration here is that young children, as well as older ones, use both the first and the second language as a thinking process.

So, what is it that you, as an adult second-language learner, can gain from looking at how children learn a second language? It seems quite evident that, in childhood, a number of first-language learning principles apply to second-language learning but also that a few conclusions have to be qualified. Principles have to be seen in perspective as you draw insights for yourself, as an adult, from the child's second-language learning process.

Four fundamental principles appear to stand out:

1. Don't worry unduly about your accent
2. Don't overanalyze yourself
3. Shed your inhibitions
4. Try not to let your native language interfere

Don't worry unduly about your accent

In Mark Twain's *The Innocents Abroad*, a French-speaking guide introduces himself: "If ze zhentlemans will to me make ze grande honneur to me rattain in hees serveece, I shall show to heem everysing zat is magnifique to look upon in ze beautiful Paree. I speaky ze Angleesh parfaitmaw."[18] You can just hear him, can't you? An accent is the most noticeable aspect of the speech of someone who hasn't learned the language as a young child. That accent usually identifies the learner's origin since the accent is overwhelmingly made up of characteristics of the native language that are *mapped* on to the second.

Most children develop authentic native accents in a second language if they've had sufficient exposure to the second language and time to use it for genuine survival. But something happens around the age of puberty. Children, now in the process of becoming adults, become significantly less able to develop completely authentic native accents in the language. Why do we have this mysterious plasticity in the younger years and where does it go? Is there some sort of linguistic hardening of the arteries?

One answer to these questions is simple. In order to produce speech, a human being uses literally several hundred tiny muscles of the throat, tongue, lips, and cheek. Like any other physical or athletic endeavor, the younger you begin this skill, the better your chances are of being adept in it. As you grow older, those muscles are more difficult to train—or, in this case, to retrain, since you've already developed habits in your native language. And soon after your first decade of life, changing those habits becomes increasingly difficult.

The problem with this line of thinking is that it doesn't necessarily explain why puberty seems to be a turning point. Why not age five? or eight? or sixteen? The answer may lie in the nature of the development of the human brain, and the essentially neuromuscular nature of human speech. According to some scientists, the brain completes the process of *lateralization*, that is, assigning functions to either the left hemisphere or the right, around the age of puberty, and a connection (albeit thin) is made between brain lateralization and the loss of neuromuscular plasticity. (We'll look more closely at right- and left-brain functions in chapter 5.)

Figure 4

There is disagreement[19] on the lateralization theory. For example, one study showed that lateralization may be complete by the age of five, while others point toward puberty as the time for completion of the process. There are some interesting anthropological studies of multilingual societies where people engage in routine second-, third-, and fourth-language learning as adults, apparently to perfection. Nevertheless, future research just might find that the maturation of the brain does, after all, explain the adult's relative inability, with a few exceptions, to develop a completely authentic native accent in a second language.

What does all this argument and fuzzy speculation say to you about your own second-language learning? First, you might ask yourself: is there anything inherently wrong with a foreign accent? In a few cases an accent has a stigmatizing effect. It marks you as an outsider or stranger in a context where you may very well want to feel you belong. And, yes, if you want to become a secret agent in a foreign country you had better be able to pass for a native (in real life, secret agents rarely learn their second languages after puberty). But for most of us, a foreign accent is just that: an accent that tells other people we are speaking in a second language.

There are many successful foreign language learners who nevertheless have marked foreign accents. Joseph Conrad, author of *Lord Jim*, *Typhoon*, and other well-known novels, is considered one of the great writers in English literature, yet English was his second language (his first was Polish, as his given name reveals: Josef Teodor Konrad Walecz Korzeniowski). Joseph Conrad had a marked foreign accent. Henry Kissinger, Maurice Chevalier, and others also come to mind—perfectly fluent, more talented in communicative ability than most native speakers of English, yet possessing an accent. Accents impede communication only when they are severely "broken"—when patterns of intonation, stress, and rhythm are excessively deviant.

On a practical level, you may wonder how important good pronunciation in the second language is for you. It is indeed important, but only up to the point where you have achieved an ability to convey your intended messages clearly. Beyond that, accent-improvement courses can easily become exercises in frustration and, perhaps, futility. The principle here, then, is *not* to try to emulate the child's accent-free acquisition process. Accept your neurological and/or muscular limitations and work instead toward clarity in speech. Then, don't fret if you aren't perfect. The important thing is that you learn to communicate clearly—in short, to survive—in the language.

Don't overanalyze yourself

Learning a foreign language is like learning tennis (or any other sport): if you think about it too much, it won't work. Like other tennis players, I frequently used to analyze some aspect of my tennis game. I'd tell myself to watch the ball, or follow through on my stroke, or shift my grip for the backhand. Before I knew it, I was analyzing myself so much I could hardly play a decent game of tennis. I was overmonitoring my actions to the extent that I was too acutely aware of myself. I finally found that I was better off just relaxing and not thinking about my tennis game. Instead, I was better served (no pun intended!) by simply focusing on my opponent or on winning the game—anything but focusing on myself.

Intellectually, children are somewhat relaxed as they play both the first- *and* second-language learning games. They don't think about the rules that they are subconsciously using and modifying daily. Instead, they focus on the goals of language use: communication with others for specific purposes. Second-language learning for children is, like first-language learning, a subconscious effort; they pick up language. And they don't watch themselves the way adults in a classroom often do.

This doesn't mean, however, that children don't work at absorbing language. They work very diligently at it. They spend hours and hours every day acquiring language. Their mental efforts are often consumed with the process; they are determined in their own subconscious way to grasp the meaning of others' language and to convey language themselves. In the younger years this effort involves only listening and speaking, and not reading and writing, which enter into the picture at school age.

Should adults also try to pick up language subconsciously? The answer is a qualified yes. We do too much analyzing of ourselves in general. If we decide we should learn a foreign language, most of us, as adults, feel we need to learn it in the context of a foreign language class. We memorize, study rules of grammar, translate from one language to the other, and do just about everything except subconsciously acquire it. We tend to learn a lot *about* the language at the expense of learning to use it. And one sure way to fail at learning a foreign language is not to use it for genuine communication.

One of my teacher trainees once asked me what methods he could use to teach his English-as-a-second-language class of six hundred people. I asked him if I heard him correctly. Yes, he said, six hundred! My response was that you can't teach that many people in an auditorium to speak a foreign language any more than you can teach the same number how to swim by placing all of them in a swimming pool. You can teach them about swimming: principles of flotation, gravity, movement through the water. You can demonstrate strokes or show films on swimming. But until those learners actually jump into the water on their own with enough space around them to practice their skill, they simply will not learn to swim. So it is in the language classroom. We tend to learn a lot about language but engage in very little meaningful practice.

Most successful adult second-language learning is untutored. It is achieved by persons who have been immersed in the foreign language environment and forced to communicate for survival. At that point they tend to focus on the purpose of language and not to think as much about the linguistic forms they are using or whether they are right or wrong. Foreign language classrooms have a hard time duplicating the urgency to communicate that comes hand in hand with living in a foreign culture.

So we adults should focus less on things about the language and more on purposes that our second language can be used to accomplish. But should we shy away entirely from some focus here and there on sound systems, grammar, vocabulary, or expressions? Certainly not. In the same way that your tennis game can be improved by an optimum amount of analysis (just enough to let you "zoom in" and look at your problem area and then quickly "zoom out" and get back to the game itself), so can your language game improve. We adults really have an advantage over young people here. We can use that optimal focusing for our own good. We're not limited to what is often a time-consuming process of learning something subconsciously by discovery.

It's not too ridiculous to conclude, therefore, that adults are potentially *superior* to children in foreign language learning, if we would only harness that ability. Research on successful language learners attributes a significant portion of adult success to optimal conscious learning: finding good self-teaching strategies and knowing what to look for. We'll get into that more in the next chapter.

Failure among adult second-language learners is frequently due to our perverse knack for letting ourselves be overwhelmed by the enormity of the task that lies before us, by all the sounds and words and rules and conventions we are going to have to learn. Rather than tackling language a little at a time and being satisfied with small steps of progress, we crack under pressure. One way to overcome this annoying hypersensitivity is to adopt learning strategies that will help us chip away bit by bit at the language.

In short, try not to think too much about the process of language learning that you are going through but be ready on occasion to zoom in and figure out what you are doing. If you can balance the two principles of focusing closely and of getting the larger picture, you will be well on your way to success.

Shed your inhibitions

A hundred college students have gathered in an auditorium at the University of Michigan. They've all responded to an advertisement asking human subjects to participate in a psychological experiment. When Professor Alexander Guiora and his colleagues step to the front of the room, they explain that one-half of the audience, randomly divided, will go to room A, and the other half to room B. The ones in room A are given a small glass of punch; in the punch are one-and-a-half ounces of vodka. Volunteers in room B get the same punch without the vodka. After a short period of time the participants in both rooms A and B are led to a large language laboratory. There everyone simultaneously takes a taped test in which they have to try to pronounce words in the Thai language (which none of the subjects know). After the test they are dismissed, with thanks and a token payment for their trouble.

Later the results of this experiment[20] are published. Guiora announces that group A did a significantly better job of pronouncing Thai words than group B. Conclusion: the alcohol lowered inhibitions, giving group A the advantage.

There is plenty to quibble about in this experiment, but it has been shown in other ways that one of the greatest blocks to adult second-language success is fear: fear of failing, fear of making a fool of yourself in front of others, fear of falling flat on your face. Because of these fears, our inhibitions intensify and we raise our defenses in order to protect our fragile egos. Adults are very good at figuring out how to avoid risking embarrassment. They sit in the back of the room, volunteer only when absolutely sure of an answer, and shun too much participation. In the real world they don't venture beyond a couple of memorized phrase-book routines, they let others translate or talk for them, and they seek the company of their compatriots.

Are children any different? You can't really say that they are totally uninhibited. Anyone who has children or remembers being one knows the inhibitions that they feel. "Gee, my hair looks awful." "I refuse to wear that shirt." "Jeff will laugh at me." "Everybody hates me." These are but a few of the sorts of things young people will say to themselves. They're quite egocentric: the world revolves around them, and the eyes of everyone are fixed upon them. This egocentricity, which starts at birth, makes children in many ways even more sensitive and self-conscious than adults.

But children, in a mysterious way, are less inhibited *linguistically* than adults. Beyond a certain sensitivity to in-group slang, children don't pay much attention to grammatical correctness and linguistic forms. Until about the age of puberty they aren't overtly aware that spoken language calls for a set of skills which are subject to criticism. They learn early in language arts classes that their written language should meet certain standards (which too often results in fluent, uninhibited young people suddenly being stifled), but spoken language remains relatively untouched by conscious, analytical awareness.

When a child tackles a foreign language, then, inhibitions or fears about linguistic failure aren't very evident. More evident is a fear of social failure, and the child subconsciously views language as an excellent tool for achieving social acceptance. A linguistic mistake—wrong verb tense, misused word, preposition error, word order problem, or whatever—is easily overlooked by the learner and usually ignored by native listeners.

We adults need to be more childlike in our emotional approach to learning a foreign language. We are far too afraid of making mistakes. Yet research shows that we literally must make mistakes if we are to learn a foreign language. Humor plays an important role here. If you can take a more relaxed, less anxious approach to language learning and laugh at yourself a bit rather than scurrying for the nearest hole to crawl into, your ability to learn will be enhanced (more on this in chapter 8). Meanwhile, just remember that one of the most refreshing things children teach you about foreign language learning is that you can fall flat on your face gracefully...well, almost gracefully.

Try not to let your native language interfere

FAMILY CIRCUS

"PJ can speak a foreign language! He's sayin' stuff I can't understand."

Figure 5

Nine-year-old John lives in bilingual Quebec and he speaks both French and English. His parents speak English in the home. Most of John's neighbors and friends speak French. John's classes at school are in both English and French, depending on the subject matter. John daily makes language switches back and forth, speaking English with his parents and family, French with neighbors and neighborhood friends, and both French and English at school.

The two languages seldom get mixed up or confused in his mind. How does he do it?

Children are remarkable in their ability to keep languages from interfering with each other. They easily associate a particular language with a context or a person. They can even do mental translation: someone comes to the door, gives an oral message in language A, the child goes to someone in the house and delivers the message in language B, gets an answer in B, and goes back to the door and gives the message in language A, with no distortion and with only a funny sort of awareness that there's something different about the way to talk to different people.

Does this dexterity apply only in cases where a child is simultaneously acquiring two languages (learning both first and second languages at the same time)? Evidently not. When a child learns a second language after learning the first language, similar patterns of noninterference are found.

Because adults tend to think about language a good deal, we try to map a new language onto our native tongue. When we learn a new word in the second language, we tend to translate it into our native language. A new grammar rule is compared to "how we say it in English." And we do the best we can with the new sound system but, by nature, fall back on our English habits. Children aren't as laden with such intellectual baggage. Their penchant for diving right into the language and their intellectual simplicity (and, before puberty, inability to perform certain abstract mental operations) frees them from the overawareness that hampers adults.

Does the knowledge of our native language have any redeeming value for second-language learning? It does indeed. The mere fact that we already know a language can in itself be helpful. There may well be analogies across the two languages that are useful, especially if the languages are in the same family, like French, Spanish, or German, all of which are historically related to English. Words and phrases may be the same or similar. So don't try to pretend that your native language isn't there. Just don't let that knowledge so pervade every aspect of learning that you can't get directly into your second language.

Turning the process upside down

Adults may be doing things backwards. Researchers seem to agree that when children learn second languages, they proceed in the following order:

1. They first establish *social relationships* by whatever means—verbal or nonverbal—that are available to them.
2. Then they focus on *communication:* developing linguistic channels of conveying feelings, wants, needs, ideas, and facts.
3. Finally, at a late stage, they become concerned about *grammatical correctness,* that is, the exactness of the language forms themselves.

Partly because of the influence of formal language instruction, adults tend to turn this pattern upside down and rank order the aspects of language learning as follows:

1. First we focus on gramatical correctness—words, rules, forms, and sounds.
2. Then we try communication, practicing sentences that eventually get used in quasi-meaningful situations.
3. Finally, having built our confidence by learning the rules and practicing communication, we go out there and try to establish social relationships.

What would happen if we turned the pattern—in the children's terms—right side up?

Some basic principles

It is clear that the process by which children learn a second language offers guidelines for adult second-language learning. Some principles have emerged from our discussion:

1. The pattern by which children learn a first or second language can be useful in facilitating adult language learning.
2. However, first-language acquisition by children is different enough from adult second-language acquisition that you need to beware of assuming that everything the child does in the native language provides a lesson for you in second-language learning. It's better to compare child second-language acquisition with adult second-language acquisition, and even then you should watch out for false analogies.
3. Whether or not innateness factors are still present, or the critical period has passed you by, you are still perfectly capable of learning a second language.
4. Don't worry about attaining a perfect nativelike accent. Clear, unambiguous pronunciation in the second language, even with a foreign accent, should be your goal.
5. Try not to think too much about the language you are learning. Some thinking is good, an adult advantage, but most of us intellectualize too much.
6. Language learning can be scary because you have to make mistakes, but kids manage not to be inhibited by linguistic mis-takes. You, too, should try to be more childlike in this sense. Don't worry about making mistakes. Try to let your defensive walls down.
7. In some ways, your native language is a monster that will always lurk in the shadows to haunt your second-language learning efforts. Try not to let it overwhelm you. Use it for analogies here and there, but remember that kids manage to free themselves fairly easily from the native language, and so should you.
8. Turn your adult tendencies upside down and put social relationships first, then communication, and only then worry about grammatical correctness. It may just work.

These are some beginning principles on which you can base your language learning strategies. As you think about these principles, you might try to relate them to your own current, prospective, or past language learning experiences. Do you worry too much about your accent? Do you analyze yourself too much? Are you inhibited? If any of the principles apply to you, how might you develop strategies for self-improvement?

The next two chapters of the book lead you toward further self-understanding and personal strategies for success. Chapter 4 lays some steppingstones toward developing an understanding of the mental (intellectual, cognitive) processes that all adults utilize in foreign language learning. Then in chapter 5 you will discover some ways in which you are different from others, which will in turn aid you in developing your own preferred pathways to success.

4

Using

Your Brain Power

Here is the sort of advertisement that's not very hard to find in magazines these days:

WHAT COULD YOU BE DOING
WITH THE UNUSED 90% OF YOUR BRAIN?

Discover your mind's potential in a weekend workshop. Most people use a very small part of their brain capacity. Imagine how your life would improve if you could tap this tremendous resource. Once you learn how to activate your brain with the internationally proven "POWER LEARN-ING" system, you can continue the process on your own for the rest of your life! With this unique system, you can assimilate material several times faster than you do now. Moreover, you'll learn it without stress.

The flyer that you would get from POWER LEARNING* goes on to give you applications of their system and, of course, those glowing testimonials from satisfied customers.

---

* A fictitious company.

Of course we are all enticed just a bit by this sort of hype. You may actually have gone through one or two of those weekend workshops. If you were lucky, you walked away with a few interesting ideas. Otherwise, you were just several hundred dollars lighter and soon lapsed back into your same old habits. Either way, it all adds up to the reality that there is no magic formula that will transport you effortlessly from your present world of mental finiteness to a universe of infinite wisdom. A long-term mind improvement process requires much more than a weekend workshop with scintillating people and slick activities.

As you begin to learn a foreign language, you wouldn't be human if you weren't lured by the thought of some quick and wonderful way to set your mind on a course that would effortlessly bestow the ability to speak the language fluently. Think how you could impress your friends! Unfortunately, foreign language learning works like other things: there is no quick and easy set of mental gymnastics that will propel you through the maze of material. No magic. No quick fix. But take heart, there are a number of insights into the human learning process that have been profitably applied to learning a foreign language. Years of research on second-language learning have identified some clear landmarks which can guide your search for success.

Let's look at some of these important fundamentals and how they might contribute to your learning a foreign language better and faster.

Running through the maze

Stories about laboratory mice are familiar to the armchair psychologist. We all know that mice learn how to run through mazes because they figure out that a little goody awaits them at the end. The applications to human behavior, in general at least, are obvious. But do psychologists' mice have anything to tell us about the complexity of human learning and memory? And even more remotely, can these simple rodents tell us anything about that most intricate of human intellectual accomplishments, the learning of a language? The answer is a rather surprising yes, as long as we recognize some limitations. Three basic principles for developing language learning strategies emerge.

The power of rewards

We are reward-governed creatures. The consequences of our behavior have ultimate importance. When we do something, we do it for the effect that it will bring. Those effects—the events that follow an action, thought, or utterance—determine the extent to which that behavior will be repeated and learned. When a baby accidentally touches a mobile hanging over her crib, she hears little tinkling bell sounds. The sounds are pleasing. After several such accidental contacts with the mobile, she connects the pleasant sounds with the movement of her arm. In due course, she willfully bats at the mobile so that she can hear the bells. Her actions are governed by pleasant consequences or rewards.

Language works the same way. Little children discover that saying certain words like *milk* or *truck* or, later on, *please* brings about certain rewards. The uttering of those words causes milk to appear, a truck to be given, or favors to be granted. When we use language, we are reinforced—rewarded—for language that either gets us what we want or evokes in us a pleasurable or positive feeling.

In learning a foreign language we are equally controlled by the consequences of our learning, because we consciously and eagerly look for little signs here and there that we have succeeded in our attempt to communicate. If you have tried learning a foreign language before, you know the pleasure you get when you say even such simple things as *"Donnez-moi la plume"* and someone actually gives you a pen.

Punishment

Psychologist B. F. Skinner[21] showed in his animal experiments that punishment had little long-term effect. He found, in fact, that mild punishment served more often as a positive reinforcer than an element that would extinguish undesirable behavior. It called attention, in a sense, to the behavior and caused the animals to continue it. Parents know that this principle is often borne out in rearing children. How many times do kids persist in throwing the spinach on the floor or using a dirty word or leaving their rooms in a horrendous mess—just for the attention they get from parents as they are scolded? Skinner found that the best way to extinguish undesirable behavior is for the experimenter to ignore it: neither reward it nor give punishment.

In foreign language learning you are likewise much better off accentuating the positive than beating yourself for your failures. While you certainly don't want to ignore your errors (you can learn a lot from them—more about that in chapter 8), you don't need to punish yourself for them. Instead, look for the rewards in what you are doing right. Notice how you learn more and more words each day. Look for the rewarding smile on the other person's face when you say something right. Pat yourself on the back for getting through today's lesson.

Emitted responses

Skinner also showed that external stimuli are not very powerful in eliciting long-term learning. He found that *emitted* responses, that is, responses that come from within the learner, were more likely to stick. For example, a mouse being taught to walk through a maze will learn the route better in the long run if it is simply allowed to make its own turns (correct ones of which would be followed by a reward) than if it is goaded, prodded, jabbed, or in some other external way stimulated to make the correct turn.

As you learn a second language you can use this principle to check yourself: are you relying too much on letting someone else—a book, a cassette program, a teacher—move you along? Some direction from the outside is helpful, but even in the early stages you ought to experience moments when you are emitting your own internal response, and not just being led along someone else's path.

Finding your mental pegs

Studies of human learning and memory show that we store things in our brain by fitting them into existing structures. I like to think of it as a process of hanging items onto mental pegs, which may be called *meaningful learning*. Learning is meaningful if your efforts attach the new behavior (or fact or feeling) to existing structures in your mind. Your memory is made up of thousands, if not millions, of categories and subcategories which are intricately interrelated like a complex system of roots.

Rote learning is just the opposite of meaningful learning. When you learn something in rote fashion, it has no peg to hang on. Often phone numbers are learned by rote for a short period of time but are not meaningfully lodged in your mind. Events that have no meaning for you are retained for a few seconds, maybe, but never get converted to your more permanent, long-term memory.

Learning a foreign language can very easily degenerate into a rote process. The sounds are new. The words are new. The sentences are new. Your hierarchies of memory have few if any pegs on which to hang the bits and pieces of your new language. What's more, if you do a lot of memorizing of words and phrases without thinking about their meaning or using them for actual communication, you just end up cluttering your mind with uncategorized bits of information. Since the human brain can only stand so much clutter, it is obviously important to find ways to keep all new aspects of the language on the meaningful side of your mental ledger.

Foreign language classes which include a lot of drilling often fail to get at that all-important meaningfulness. The reason is that the new language is being learned by rote, not being integrated into the whole system of thinking. Instead, it is forced to occupy a separate little compartment out in the middle of nowhere. And when you keep trying to fill that limited compartment with more drilled words and sentences, the memorized material doesn't get channeled into your main system.

When I was practice-teaching a high school French class, I was amused by the comments of a proud mother at parents night early in the year. "Oh, Mr. Brown," she said, "I'm so amazed at my daughter's conversational ability in French! Why, after just one week of your teaching she now talks to her classmate on the telephone in French!" Well, I knew there was some mistake. Those were the days when it was fashionable to spend most of the class hour doing rote dialogue memorization, and her daughter's "conversations" turned out to be a mere parroting of her daily memorized dialogues.

For language to become meaningful, it must be used in real communication in relatively unrehearsed situations. Don't box up your foreign language in its rehearsed context of memorized drills and routines. Open it up and let it be used for what it was intended—to communicate.

Defensive learning

Go back for a moment and picture yourself in your elementary school or high school. How much of your learning resulted from competing against your schoolmates, trying to outdo them in the grade-getting game? How much came from trying to please your teachers by doing what they told you to do? And how much was a product of following the rules, meeting state requirements, and passing standardized tests? For many of us, too much of our learning in school was defensive. We learned to defend ourselves against the competition of other learners, the teacher, and the institution. This set up motives for learning that were upside down. Instead of learning for its positive benefits, we kept up the pace just to avoid punishments in their various manifestations.

The learning of a foreign language is not enhanced by a defensive approach. Language is a tool for communication, for social bonding, for cooperation and understanding. It is unlikely that anyone ever learned a foreign language with wholly defensive motivations. One of the reasons that foreign language requirements in schools and universities often produce failures is that students pursue language study for the wrong motives: they want to meet a requirement rather than use the language for practical purposes. Such artificial motivation hardly spurs one to reach communicative fluency.

Look for genuine personal rewards in learning a foreign language. Rejoice in the little things that you are able to do, bit by bit, in the language. The last thing you should do is worry about whether someone sitting next to you is better at it. If you are presently in a foreign language class, you might encourage its members to come together as a group and help each other. One person's weakness may be another's strength.

Figure 6

You and your language learning IQ

How does the concept of intelligence fit into the picture? Is there some relationship between intelligence and successful second-language learning? Or can "any old dummy" learn a second language?

Traditionally, intelligence has been defined and measured in terms of *verbal* and *logical-mathematical* abilities. Our concept of IQ (intelligence quotient) is based on several generations of testing of these two abilities, stemming from the research of Alfred Binet in the early years of this century. Statistics show that success in educational and academic endeavors is directly related to IQ. In terms of meaningful learning, high intelligence must imply a very efficient process of storing items into conceptual hierarchies in such a way that they are easily recalled.

But how good or, perhaps more precisely, how useful are those IQ tests? In looking at the process of second-language learning a curious little paradox emerges. Research has shown that, as traditionally measured by IQ tests, intelligence is not strongly linked to successful language learning. In other words, so-called brilliant people—scientific and literary geniuses and the like—aren't by any means universally brilliant second-language learners. In fact, anecdotal

evidence has turned up many an intellectual whiz who has completely failed to learn a second language. On the other side of the
coin, there is ample evidence of people of rather average intelligence—again, as measured by IQ tests—who have excelled in
mastering a foreign language.

So, what is happening here? Obviously the learning of a language is an enormous undertaking. A system of tens of thousands of
words that can be ordered in an infinite number of sequences is no
small matter for the brain to deal with effectively. Memory carries
a particularly heavy burden, for we have to retain this system in
some orderly way so that appropriate subsystems can be recalled in
the many contexts that we face daily. The traditional concept of
IQ is too limited to explain or measure everything that is going on.
Our "language learning IQs" appear to be very complicated mecha-
nisms, not merely confined to the two traditional IQ factors.

Frames of mind

Psychologist Howard Gardner is one of several people recently
who have found limitations in those traditional measurements of
intelligence. In *Frames of Mind*,[22] Gardner notes that the IQ concept
has unduly narrowed our notion of intelligence. There is much more,
he says, to mental capacity than what we have been given to believe.
In a somewhat controversial theory of intelligence, Gardner describes
not two, but seven different forms of knowing, which, in his view,
give us a more comprehensive picture of intelligence. Beyond the
two traditional measures, Gardner adds five more to complete his
description of human intelligence:

1. Linguistic intelligence
2. Logical or mathematical intelligence
3. Spatial intelligence (the ability to find your way around an
   environment, to form mental images of reality, and to
   transform them readily)

4. Musical intelligence (the ability to perceive and create pitch and rhythmic patterns)
5. Bodily or kinesthetic intelligence (fine-motor movement, athletic prowess)
6. Interpersonal intelligence (the ability to understand others, how they feel, what motivates them, and how they interact with one another)
7. Intrapersonal intelligence (the ability to see oneself, to develop a sense of self-identity)

Gardner maintains that by looking only at the first two categories we rule out a great number of mental abilities. Moreover, he shows that our traditional definitions of intelligence are culture bound. The sixth sense of a hunter in New Guinea or the navigational abilities of a sailor in Micronesia are not accounted for in our Westernized definitions of IQ.

By broadly defining intelligence as Gardner has done, we can more easily discern a relationship between intelligence and second-language learning. Among his seven factors are mental attributes that are crucial to second-language success. Musical intelligence explains the relative ease with which some learners perceive and produce tones and rhythm that carry a great deal of meaning in all languages. Bodily or kinesthetic intelligence contributes to the ability to pick up the pronunciation of a language and to improve one's accent. Interpersonal intelligence—the way we perceive and understand other people—is of paramount importance in the communication process. Intrapersonal factors (see chapter 6) are crucial to the development of self-esteem and of social transactional strategies, which are essential foundation stones for building foreign language competence. We could even speculate on the extent to which spatial intelligence, especially a sense of direction, may assist the second-culture learner in becoming comfortable in new surroundings.

It is not at all hard to see now why Mensa Society members may not necessarily be the best language learners: there is much more to the intellectual process of language learning than the IQ-oriented world would lead us to believe. Those "brains" back in school may be using just two-sevenths of their brains.

Three heads are better than one

Gardner's concept of intelligence is liberating and gratifying to those who feel somewhat inferior because they couldn't master IQ tests (and other tests of that ilk) that are highly focused, standardized, and timed. Now we can take heart that some psychologists are beginning to recognize broader definitions of intelligence.

Yale professor Robert Sternberg is among those who join Gardner in the liberation. In *Beyond IQ*,[23] Sternberg describes three kinds of test takers:

1. Alice is a whiz at test taking and analytical thinking.
2. Barbara isn't a super test taker, but she's superior in the kind of creative thinking in which widely different experiences are interrelated.
3. Celia doesn't do too well in tests, but she's street-smart. She has learned how to "play the game" and to manipulate her environment.

Sternberg's point is that IQ and other standardized tests don't measure all of the intellectual skills that people use in order to succeed.

Successful second-language learners are often "Barbaras" and "Celias." They succeed not because of a superior capacity to analyze a problem but because they can take words, phrases, rules, and sentences and put them to use intuitively. And they have learned something about game playing (see chapter 6 for more on this) that enables them to get what they need through the vehicle of language.

The work of Sternberg and Gardner expands our concept of mental functioning and encourages language learners to take a broader view of language aptitude. You may not be able to increase that aptitude in a quickie weekend workshop like the one described at the beginning of this chapter, but through a deliberate process of concentration, some of your mental skills can indeed grow in quality. By understanding your own intellectual strengths and weaknesses in a variety of categories, you can go about the language learning task, capitalize on those strengths that keep you successful, and work to improve on those areas where your weaknesses may be holding you back. The next chapter will deal further with specific learning and thinking styles that are beneficial.

Superlearning

A man walks briskly to the back of an auditorium filled with nuclear scientists, some of them Russia's most brilliant. Mikhail Keuni, an artist, tells a volunteer on the stage, "Turn that big blackboard around so that it is facing away from me. Take a piece of chalk and cover the blackboard with circles. They can intersect. They can be inside one another. Draw them any way you wish." The volunteer madly draws dozens of circles. As the board is spun around for Keuni to glance at it, the audience laughs. It is white with circles. Keuni's eyes scarcely blink. In two seconds he calls out the total, 167! Five minutes of careful calculation by the audience verifies Keuni's answer.[24]

Reportedly Keuni was similarly able to channel his "superlearning" abilities toward language acquisition. When his tour plans called for a trip to Japan, he is said to have become completely fluent in Japanese in one month. Later, a trip to Finland prompted him to master Finnish in a week.

What accounts for such incredible mental powers? Do people like Keuni have an innate set of neurological capacities that are simply unique? Or did Keuni go to one of those "Power Learning" workshops? Can ordinary people like us avail ourselves of what we might think of as superhuman abilities that have heretofore been hidden from us? Experts say that we only use a small fraction of our brain capacity. Is there some way to release a significantly greater fraction?

These questions, hinted at in the beginning of this chapter, might be answered in the light of a variety of *superlearning*[25] techniques for getting bunches of things stuffed into your brain in a short time. We can now look at this research against the backdrop of other facts about human memory that have already been touched on here.

Some psychologists are convinced that there are indeed valid methods that can be employed to increase dramatically the learning capacity of our brains. One of the better known experimenters in this quest is the Bulgarian Georgi Lozanov, who believes that superlearning power is a natural human ability, available to anyone who will work hard enough to achieve it. Through his method of *Suggestology*, students are put into relaxed states of consciousness, with quiet music playing in the background, and then given large quantities of various forms of subject matter: math, physics, history, language. Lozanov's experiments claim phenomenal results: in 1977 one report claimed that foreign language students had absorbed as many as three thousand words a day in Suggestology classes.[26]

Suggestology has been applied to foreign language classes all over Europe and the United States. There are claims that the method, sometimes called "Suggestopedia," will provide an enormous increase in vocabulary knowledge and even in conversational ability. Lozanov capitalizes on the principle that the brain is most receptive in the presleep phase during which pulse and blood pressure decrease and alpha brain waves increase. In "relaxed concentration" we are "restfully alert" and able to take in large amounts of data that we otherwise block out. We will look more closely at a typical Suggestopedia class in a foreign language in chapter 9.

Lozanov's contentions about learning are the same as those used by Suzuki in teaching music, where students go to sleep at night listening to tapes of the music they are learning to play. Transcendental meditation induces similar neurophysiological changes; in fact, Lozanov derived many of his insights from a study of yoga practice in India. "Sleep teaching" tapes have had a recent resurgence. Keep in mind, though, that sleep teaching is a bit of a misnomer. The key is to take in the material just prior to going to sleep, when conditions are optimal and before you lapse into unconsciousness. Art Linkletter is reported to have learned some Mandarin Chinese through ten nights of sleep learning, enough Chinese, anyway, to cause the vice-consul of China to compliment him on his perfectly conversant knowledge of Chinese (we aren't told how much the vice-consul was influenced by the cultural habit of Chinese to compliment their guests, however).

Can you learn a foreign language by sitting in a comfortable chair, relaxing, and listening to tapes of people pronouncing words and engaging in conversations? To some extent. It will at least provide some crucial input that will later become a part of your conscious storehouse of knowledge in the language. Suggestopedia sessions with do-it-yourself, home-study tapes may indeed help you. Don't rule out the possibility just because it sounds a little bizarre.

But, at the same time, beware. Often, the descriptions of these methods fail to tell you all the other things you have to do to make them work. The Lozanov experiments in Bulgaria included other activities that accompanied the taped "concert" sessions: exercises, role plays, written work, conversation practice. Neither Art Linkletter, Mikhail Keuni, nor anyone else masters a language simply by listening to presleep tapes. They use the language in meaningful communication. They apply many forms of intelligence, especially interpersonal intelligence, to the process of language learning.

The bottom line, then, is that supermemory and superlearning abilities may be available to you, and they could well enhance your total learning effort. Don't rule out any possibility until you've made an effort to make it work. At the same time, you would do well to respect a storehouse of research indicating that many of these experimental methods have been oversold and have made promises they cannot keep. Keuni and others really are extraordinary individuals and ordinary people like you and me shouldn't hold them up as our models any more than we should believe that a weekend workshop is guaranteed to turn our lives around.

Forgetting and how to prevent it

Superlearning has come to be associated with the rapid intake of information, but what good would that intake be if you couldn't remember it? The opposite of learning is forgetting. How can we prevent it?

People disagree on just what forgetting is. Psychologists have been arguing about it for years. Do you ever really forget anything once you know it? Or are those little brain cells always there but simply hiding in some shadowy corner of your mind? Every day thousands of perceptions enter your brain: you see people on sidewalks and cars in the streets; your ears hear music, news, and talk shows; you read tens of thousands of words in the newspaper. Yet you don't remember most of these items. What happens to those brain cells that aided in the perceptions? Maybe they are like magnetic tapes that record images and meanings for fleeting moments, only to be erased by the next wave of perceived images.

But what about those things that you "knew" at one point but then later could not bring back? Do they get erased in the same way? If so, why do certain associations trigger these memories? Say you lived in some town many years ago. For the life of you, you can't remember street names or the names of many of your acquaintances. After twenty years you go back and suddenly your physical presence in the old neighborhood subconsciously brings memories to the forefront of your mind.

"Forgotten" languages behave in much the same way. There are many reports of people who were once quite fluent in a second language but who lost that fluency through years of disuse. But thrust them into the environment where they learned the language, and suddenly their fluency is intact. It "comes back to you," they say. Where were all those brain cells during the years the language was forgotten? Maybe that's why we only use 10 percent of our brain: the rest of it is a storehouse with doors tightly locked, and only certain keys will unlock them.

Some fascinating experiments have been done to determine the extent to which forgotten childhood languages can be recalled under hypnosis. Unfortunately, the findings haven't been very revealing. Subjects have recalled certain phrases and expressions in hypnotic states but little more.

Can you, in your quest for foreign language skills, maximize your retention capacity and somehow find ways to avoid the seemingly inevitable process of forgetting? The key is meaningful learning. If an item is truly lodged or (as some psychologists say) "subsumed" into your mental structure, you have a very hard time forgetting it because it becomes an integral part of a larger mental pattern. It "fits," and without it a particular mental system is incomplete in some way. We easily forget information learned by rote because it doesn't fit. Flash cards and lists of words that we try to memorize in a foreign language often remain in the rote learning category. They don't get attached to a growing network of language experience and meaning. To avoid forgetting, then, you have to make the language you are learning as meaningful as possible (and, of course, you have to use it). How do you do that?

Create communicative urgency

When you fail to learn a foreign language, it is usually because you don't have situations confronting you daily where communicative urgency is at work, that is, a situation in which you must convey messages in the language for purposes of your own survival. When you don't have to learn something, you often don't learn it. The motivation isn't there, or it's there only in a somewhat artificial or defensive way: you want a good grade, you want to please your teacher or your family. For many of us in the U.S., there are no readily available situations of communicative urgency. But you can make your own quasi-urgent motives for language learning. Plan a trip to the foreign country where the language is spoken and keep away from all the other American tourists. Go on a student exchange semester abroad. Live in a "foreign language" house. Insist on speaking only the foreign language with someone you know who speaks it.

Practice using the language

If you can't easily find a genuine context with built-in communicative urgency, your next best step toward meaningfulness is at least to practice using the foreign language in some context, however artificial. With a fellow learner, a foreign visitor, an exchange student in your home, or at a language club in a school, you can find people to converse with. In these cases you can still achieve some meaningfulness because you are making a concerted attempt to put the bits and pieces of language together in a coherent, structured way. If your conversation is unrehearsed—not merely memorized phrases and sentences from a lesson book—no matter how brief or trivial, it will contribute to the building of a mental network in the foreign language.

Play with language

Meaningfulness often comes when you manipulate language. Treat it like a game (more on this in chapter 6) in which every statement you make tests a little hypothesis in your mind about how the language works. If your hunch isn't right, then you can try again. As you keep making guesses and experimenting with words and phrases and as you receive feedback from those you are conversing with, you achieve meaningfulness because you have made the language your own. You haven't just swallowed somebody else's rules and then made blind attempts to apply them.

Manufacture meaningfulness

Sometimes, when all the attempts to communicate and practice and play with language still seem to leave you feeling a bit inadequate, you need to try what Frank Smith[27] calls "manufacturing meaningfulness." Through various memory games and gimmicks you can make up word associations or mnemonic patterns to hold something in your memory. This makes use of the principle of association. When you first encounter a word you don't know, do something with the word. Novice musicians remember the musical notes of the staff lines of the treble clef with the unforgettable "Every Good Boy Does Fine." Such devices stick in the mind better than unconnected letters. I could never remember how to spell *supersede* until one day I invented a story about a brilliant farmer who developed super seeds, and thereafter I remembered to use an *s* where I was inclined to put a *c*.

In second-language learning you sometimes have to work at making a vocabulary word stick. You shouldn't shy away from inventing certain associations to help you. Cognates (words that have the same root in two languages) can help. *Livre* is "book" in French; the English cognate *library* may trigger the association. Robert Blair[28] describes a unique system for learning Russian. He reduces Russian phrases to *English* words that *sound* like Russian. For example, if you want to say "hello" in Russian, you say *z-drahvst-voo-eet-yeh*. Blair suggests that this rather difficult string of syllables can be relatively easily retained by remembering instead four English words: "straws to witch ya." "My name is...," which in Russian is *meen-yah zah-voot*, becomes "mean jaws a boot." With this rather wacky mnemonic creativity, Blair suggests that we can expand our retention greatly. Don't knock it until you've tried it!

Practice selective forgetting

It may seem contradictory in the midst of a treatise on remembering to include a recommendation to practice forgetting. But the selective forgetting of the unnecessary can contribute greatly to learning what is important. We have to forget some things in order to protect ourselves from mental overcrowding.

When you were a child, you probably had dozens of experiences—both actual and linguistically symbolic—with things that burn: fires, stoves, irons, matches, candles, and so on. Through the buildup of these experiences you developed a concept of heat and of heat sufficient to burn and hurt you. But then you forgot almost all of the specific instances. You selectively pruned these minutiae, leaving only a general concept of the properties of heat. In other words, you swept your mind of cluttering details.

With language we don't need to remember every word or conversation and certainly not every rule that we encounter. Don't try to remember too many definitions, too many grammar rules, too many translations, or too many of the things teachers or books tell you about language. If for a period of time a rule or mnemonic device or translation helps, that's okay. But then you need to prune the devices and specific instances where rules apply and retain the deeper impressions of meaning and use.

Learning how to learn

If there was some doubt before you read this chapter about whether there are any principles of learning that you can apply in your efforts at second-language acquisition, I hope it is now dispelled. While we adults need to relax a bit more with language learning and cultivate some of the attitudes that help children acquire languages, there is a lot we can do to chart our own course toward success. Among them:

1. Remember the power of rewards.
2. Don't punish yourself.
3. Try to generate your own language as much as possible, and avoid relying on others to elicit it from you.
4. Attach learning meaningfully to what you know.
5. Don't engage in defensive learning where your motivation is simply to avoid certain punishments.
6. Keep in mind that intelligence, as we traditionally think of it, may not be a big factor in your success. Newer, broader theories of intelligence suggest that many intellectual capacities can be tapped in learning a second language.
7. Remember that you don't have to be a whiz at the standardized test game in order to be a good language learner.
8. Experiment with relaxation exercises and tapes and see if some material sinks in, but don't expect to achieve fluency in a language through superlearning. Much more is needed.
9. Prevent forgetting with meaningful communication, practice, play, associations, and, believe it or not, selective forgetting.

5

STRATEGIES
FOR SUCCESS

Look at the three puzzles on the next page. Take a few minutes to try to solve each of them. If you aren't very fond of doing little puzzles like this, that's okay. Just play with them for a while. Don't give up if the answers don't come to you right away—they don't to most people. You may need to think about them awhile and come back to them later. Do give them a try before looking up the answers at the end of this chapter on pages 72. The process you use in your attempts to solve them has some bearing on how you tackle a foreign language.

When you think you have solved the puzzles, or you are just ready to look at the answers and move on, engage in a little introspection: try to recall the different steps you took to reach your solutions. What were some of the hunches or hypotheses you tried out? Did you test quite a few hypotheses in rather rapid succession or did you first try to discover an overall pattern? Did you focus closely on details? Did you see what was relevant, or did some things distract you? Did you stay with the process until you reached a solution, or did you peek at the answers?

Puzzle #1

Fill in the sixth piece of the pie:

Puzzle #2

Decipher the message below:

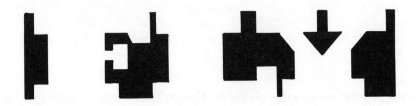

Puzzle #3

How can you plant a total of ten trees in five rows of four trees each?

Figure 7

After you have thought a little bit about how you went about trying to solve the puzzles, you might give them to some friends and see how they do. Compare their strategies with your own. You will probably find that some of their strategies were similar to yours and others were different; yet, they led you all to the same correct (or incorrect) conclusions.

In the first puzzle you had to look for a system of some kind, something that would define relationships among the symbols in the six pieces in the pie. The key was to find out what those symbols really were. You probably immediately assumed they were all just letters of the alphabet. You imposed a well-known system onto the puzzle, unaware at that point that a somewhat lesser-used system (Roman numerals) had to be used to interpret three of the symbols. Second-language learning is like that. We impose our native language system onto the second and assume wherever possible that there will be direct carryover. Sometimes there isn't.

The second puzzle may be a total mystery until you figure out what to look for. You probably started working on the black blotches at first, relatively unaware of the space in between, which turned out to be the relevant factor.

The third puzzle is a bit too "IQ-test-like" for some of us and like the subjunctive mood in French or the Chinese writing system, it seems impossible to get. Then, when you finally do get it, you wonder why you found it so hard to solve.

The strategies we employ in solving puzzles like these are partly a result of differing styles. In the case of the puzzles, we see them as problem-solving styles, but we can just as easily understand them as cognitive styles or ways in which we perceive, store, process, and retrieve information. Learning a foreign language is really a process of finding a series of solutions to problems. As you try to learn the language, your "problem" is the language, which in turn is broken down into a million subproblems—learning the words, the rules for stringing words together, the pronunciation patterns, and so forth. How you gather, store, process, and use information greatly influences your approach to learning a language.

The manner in which you solve problems doesn't apply just to paper and pencil puzzles and language idiosyncrasies. Suppose you are visiting a foreign country where you don't speak or read the language. You have landed in the airport and your contact person, whose name you don't know, is not there to meet you. To top it off, your luggage is missing. It is three o'clock in the morning and no one in the sparsely staffed airport speaks English. What will you do? There is obviously no single solution to this multifaceted problem. Your reaction will be based to a great extent on how you approach the problem. For example, if you are somewhat tolerant of ambiguity, you won't get easily flustered by your unfortunate circumstances. If you are reflective, you will exercise patience and not jump quickly to a conclusion about how to approach the situation. If you are field sensitive, you'll focus on the whole picture, and not be distracted by the surrounding but irrelevant details.

Your personal characteristics of thinking, analyzing, or problem solving distinguish you from other people. We each have unique ways of taking in information, digesting it, and recalling it for later use. These differences are the primary reason why educational institutions have to pay attention to the individualization of instruction: we don't all learn things in the same way. As we explore some of these differences, try to figure out what your own particular styles are. You will then get a sense of how you can capitalize on your uniqueness, use a variety of techniques drawing on both sides of the brain, and develop your own personal pathway to success.

Getting into your right mind

We observed in chapter 3 that as the child's brain matures, various functions become lateralized to the left or the right hemisphere. The left hemisphere is associated with logical, analytical thought, and with mathematical and linear processing of information. The right hemisphere perceives and remembers visual, tactile, and auditory images, and is more efficient in processing holistic, integrative, and emotional information. The differences between right- and left-brain functioning comprise a whole set of cognitive (thinking) style differences. The chart below lists some of the characteristics of left- and right-brain functioning.[29]

Left-Brain Dominance	Right-Brain Dominance
Intellectual	Intuitive
Remembers names	Remembers faces
Responds to verbal instructions and explanations	Responds to demonstrated, illustrated or symbolic instructions
Experiments systematically and with control	Experiments randomly and with limited restraint
Makes objective judgments	Makes subjective judgments
Planned and structured	Fluid and spontaneous
Prefers established, defined information	Prefers elusive, undefined information
Analytic reader	Synthesizing reader
Reliance on language in thinking and remembering	Reliance on images in thinking and remembering
Prefers talking and writing	Prefers drawing and manipulating objects
Prefers multiple choice tests	Prefers open-ended questions
Controls feelings	Free with feelings
Not good at interpreting body language	Good at interpreting body language
Rarely uses metaphors	Frequently uses metaphors
Favors logical problem solving	Favors intuitive problem solving

In recent years we have seen a flurry of interest in left- and right-brain functioning. Books like Betty Edwards' *Drawing on the Right Side of the Brain*,[30] for example, garnered some attention as would-be artists tried to extricate themselves from left-brain methods of imaging and visualizing their subject matter. In Japan, Tsunoda's *The Japanese Brain*[31] asserted the uniqueness of hemispheric functioning among the Japanese. In a series of experiments, Tsunoda found what he felt were marked differences between Japanese and people of other nationalities (even Chinese and Koreans) in their left- and right-brain functioning. Some of his followers have gone so far as to claim that the uniqueness of the Japanese brain is to blame for inadequate English language mastery by the Japanese. At the same time, Edwards and others contend that most Westerners are too left-brained—too analytical, too systematic, too structured. However, much of this sort of work remains rather speculative in nature.

While there may be many differences between left- and right-brain characteristics, it is important to remember that the left and right hemispheres operate together as a team. Messages are sent back and forth in such a way that both hemispheres are involved in much of the neurological activity of the human brain. Most learning contexts involve the capacities of both hemispheres, and often the best solutions to problems are those in which each hemisphere has participated optimally.

Nevertheless, we all tend to have one hemisphere that is more dominant. If, for example, you tend to remember images and visual information better than linguistic and verbal information, you'll prefer attaching your second-language experiences to visual, charted, graphic images, and possibly to body language rather than just relying on your linguistic memory alone.

Research studies[32] on second-language learning and hemispheric functioning have come up with an interesting finding. People learning second languages in natural environments (that is, not in the classroom) appear to do more right-brain processing in the early stages than in the more advanced stages of learning. It may be that our natural tendency is to absorb language at the outset and then to become more analytical in the later stages of the learning process. Most of our foreign language classes do just the opposite: they teach the nuts and bolts from the outset and then hope that by the third year or so people can let go as they get a feel for the language. As we saw at the end of chapter 3, once again here's an indication that we have probably been teaching language backwards.

In your foreign language learning experience, you are likely to favor the left side of your brain, which results in overanalyzing and focusing too much on details instead of backing off and allowing your intuition, spontaneity, and synthesizing capacities to take over. Your efforts would be better directed at "getting into your right mind." In the end, what you want to do is maintain a balance between your right and left brain. Use both hemispheres in that all-important team effort.

"Find the hidden monkeys in the jungle"

Remember the cereal boxes that had those wonderful puzzles on the back? One of them was a picture of a forest scene with trees and flowers and vines with the directions: "Find the hidden monkeys in the jungle." If you looked carefully, you soon began to spot them—some upside down, some sideways—a dozen or so monkeys, all camouflaged by the lines of what at first sight looked like just leaves and trees. The quickness and efficiency with which you found the monkeys reflected your ability to be *field independent,* that is, your ability to perceive a particular item or factor independently, in a field of distracting items. In the proverb, "They cannot see the forest for the trees," field independence is the ability to focus on the trees and not be distracted by the surrounding forest.

While field independence is your ability to distinguish parts from a whole, field dependence, or stated differently, *field sensitivity,* is your ability to see the whole picture, the whole forest, the larger view, or the general configuration of a problem or event. Field sensitivity is obviously as important as field independence. When you look at a painting in an art museum, it may be as important, depending on your purposes, to back off and get a sense of the whole painting—its gestalt, the complete message of the artist—as it is to look closely at the brush strokes, the technique of the painter. When you need to gain a global understanding of a complex problem, you need to move away from analysis of details and use a field-sensitive style.

It has been found that individuals usually have a tendency to favor one side or the other of the field independence/sensitivity continuum, even though some people appear to be equally comfortable with both. Depending on which way you lean, your approach to tackling problems will vary. If your strength is field independence, you will focus more carefully on the details of a situation than on the general picture. At the scene of a car accident you would note carefully the positions of the cars, the exact damage done, and so forth. If your dominant tendency is toward field sensitivity, you might overlook some of the minute details but grasp an overall picture of how the accident occurred and have some good intuitions about who may have been at fault.

In learning a foreign language your place on the independence/
sensitivity continuum will make a difference. If you generally favor field
independence, you will most likely tend to focus on the details of
language: noun and verb endings, nuances of meanings of words, rules
of how language works, and so forth. If you are field sensitive, you will
probably do better at understanding the meaning of longer stretches of
language (paragraphs, conversations). You will be more interested in
what people try to convey than in the bits and pieces (sounds, words) of
language that they use to convey it. In other words, you will look for the
big picture.

Most of us tend to be too field independent in our approach to
foreign languages—that's one big difference between children and
adults. Children don't focus on the forms of a foreign language as they
are learning it. They back off and take in larger meanings. As an adult,
you might think about whether or not you focus too closely on the "trees"
of your language and fail to see the all-important "forest" out there.

It is important for you to understand that successful language
learners are able to use both approaches when needed, which may
imply overcoming your dominant tendency. There are times when you
need to focus on details, to tackle some grammatical rules, or to check
definitions. At other times the rules need to be put on a shelf as you go
after the business of using language to grasp messages and meanings.

This need to be *bicognitive* in learning was dramatically illustrated
in the case of a Yugoslavian immigrant. When sixteen-year-old Alex and
his family emigrated from Yugoslavia, the U.S. was their final destina-
tion. However, they lived in France one year before moving to New
York. During that year in France Alex studied English systematically and
indefatigably. He read books on phonetics, studied the English sound
system, mastered English linguistics, and listened ad nauseam to records
and tapes designed to teach English pronunciation. Despite his gre-
gariousness, during the stay in France he socialized very little outside his
family.

At last the day came when he arrived in New York. Elated with his
new surroundings, he immediately put his studies aside and let his
gregarious nature go to work. He socialized with Americans at every
opportunity and got a job in a restaurant, where he had ample

opportunity to practice his English. During this time he never touched his phonetics books or records. Three years later, at age twenty, he became a student at the University of Illinois and was the subject of a case study in a graduate linguistics seminar. When tapes of his speech were played in the seminar, we were completely fooled at first. We swore we were listening to someone who had been born and raised in Brooklyn!

Your journey to proficiency may not be as dramatic. But it could easily incorporate elements of Alex's secret of success: flexibility.

Coping with chaos

How do you cope with situations that are confusing and chaotic? Do you usually freak out and search for an immediate way to extricate yourself? Or do you more calmly accept the confusion and assume that eventually there will be a way to account for it all? Answers to these questions may tell you something about how best to tackle learning a foreign language. Research has shown that persons who can tolerate ambiguity, which is actually in itself another cognitive style, are usually better language learners than those who cannot.

We are surrounded daily by ambiguity: information and feelings that are unclear or vague and that don't fall easily into our mental categories. Children, especially, see many things in the world around them that they don't fully understand: a flick of a switch turns a light on; stars shine at night but not in the daytime; rockets go up but apples fall down. Very young children are by necessity tolerant of all this ambiguity, so much so that contradictions often don't trouble their rich imaginations. As we grow older, we grow less tolerant of the ambiguity around us because we are capable of understanding more of the laws of the universe and of human nature. We therefore expect things to have logical, scientific, or philosophical explanations. Indeed, much of our intellectual enterprise is directed at converting ambiguity into knowledge that fits our understanding.

But the universe is full of ambiguity that even adults can't resolve. Think of the many things you don't understand fully: a political issue, a scientific law, a chemical formula, a social philosophy, or the workings of a microwave oven. More to the point, communication events are also part of the sea of ambiguity that you have to navigate daily. You have to make sense out of what you read in the newspaper, see through a salesperson's pitch, or read between the lines of the sob story your teenager gives you about needing twenty dollars. Often, getting the whole story is not a simple matter.

Your general intellectual or emotional tolerance level will determine how you handle all this. Some people need to have things fit into clear mental categories; they also tend to be reflective, favoring a slow, methodical approach to solving problems. Reflective people like to be certain of themselves before venturing answers or solutions. In the extreme, such people tend to be dogmatic and to think categorically.

On the other side of the continuum are those learners who are flexible and comfortable with ambiguity. Such people also usually make good mental gamblers. Because language for them doesn't need to be tied up in neat packages, they are willing to experiment with new ideas, make impulsive guesses which may be wrong. At the end of this continuum are people that are so comfortable with ambiguity that they seem incapable of having a systematic thought. In between are those who can think concretely and fit their knowledge into preestablished categories but who at the same time can function effectively in situations where the categories simply don't work.

Ambiguity tolerance is something like the old holding patterns around busy airports. A plane may not be able to land right at the moment, but it isn't sent away just because it doesn't fit in right now. It is allowed to circle, and in due course the control tower will let it land.

How do you handle the ambiguity of learning a second language? What about all those words you don't know? rules you haven't grasped? social niceties that escape you? Most of us tend to be a bit intolerant when we study a foreign language. We want everything to fit into familiar patterns, usually those of our native language. We may also struggle through sentences punctuated by long pauses while we search for the right word or inflection before moving on. Surmounting that desire for the familiar and the totally correct is a major goal in second-language learning. Don't let what you don't understand get you down.

Don't yield to the temptation to throw it all out just because it doesn't fit. After all, your mind is like a parachute: it only works when it's open.

"But how," you may be asking, "do you put ambiguity into a mental holding pattern?" The answer is: by understanding your own limitations and trying not to cram everything into your head all at once. Take things a step at a time. Find your own pace. If some grammatical point won't sink in, let it go for a few days and come back to it. If those fifty words you are supposed to learn this week are too many, cut them down to twenty-five and save the others for later.

On the other hand, you need to be careful that you aren't so tolerant—so wishy-washy—that nothing is ever brought in for a landing. Similarly, although a modicum of impulsiveness, a willingness to be wrong, is very helpful in learning a language, too much of it can also work against you. As you blurt out one wild guess after another, you may not only fracture the language beyond recognition but also delude yourself into thinking that you don't need to develop a system at all.

Information gathering

There are two distinctly different ways in which people gather information. One is called *preceptive* and the other *receptive,* and they offer another approach to understanding the significance of ambiguity tolerance. Preceptive information gatherers begin with a preconceived system for organizing and evaluating information. They start out solving a problem by trying to find elements that fit into their existing systems and tend to be intolerant of those that don't fit, that is, those that are ambiguous. Receptive people, on the other hand, are less inclined to try to fit facts into a scheme at the outset. They gather discrete bits of information without making immediate judgments on how they fit into a systematic whole.

Sherlock Holmes had a receptive information-gathering style. He collected disparate and seemingly disconnected pieces of information and refused to fit them together until he knew he had a solution to the crime. A premature, preceptive conclusion could lead in the wrong direction—as it invariably did when Dr. Watson offered a solution—and close off possibilities too soon.

In foreign language learning, of course, our preconceived system is our native language. We assume—preceptively—that if English nouns become plural by adding an *s* or *es*, so do nouns in the language we are learning. We discover very quickly that such is not the case and that we need to gather information receptively about how nouns are formed. Conclusion? Cultivate a receptive style in language learning. On the other hand, be ready to discover the system into which the facts of the target language fit. Every language has a system, it is simply different from yours. Holmes discovered the system—the unknown reality—into which his information fit, and that is what enabled him to solve the crime.

Holmes also had an arsenal of strategies he used as a detective— and that's what this book is all about: helping you discover an arsenal of strategies for solving the puzzles of language learning. Within that framework of strategies you need to be as receptive as possible in holding on to the ambiguous, mysterious elements of language with the expectation that those bits and pieces will eventually find their way into a logical, comprehensible system.

Leonard Bernstein: Successful language learner

Achieving the optimum on any of the continua we've discussed is not easy. Sherlock Holmes, for instance, while admirably receptive in his information-gathering style, was reflective in the extreme and might not have fared well had he tried to become a linguist. The late Leonard Bernstein, on the other hand, managed to combine the best of his reflectiveness and intuition. As a renowned musician, he of course traveled abroad frequently, and when he did so, he always tried to learn some of the language of the country he was visiting.

Before a trip, Bernstein's[33] strategy was to spend an hour a day for forty days, by himself, studying a phrase book. His aim was to master a basic vocabulary of about five hundred words. He concentrated on words that he would need to use in such places as hotels ("soap," "towel," and "bathroom," but *not* "ceiling," wall," and "floor," which he wouldn't be likely to use) and restaurants ("glass," "knife," "wine," and "check"). He didn't worry about the names of flowers and animals that he would have no use for. He studied verbs only in their simplest form. Of these, he learned the endings for just a few of the most common. One of these was always the word for "want." That way he could say things like "I want to buy...," "He wants to order...," "They want to go...," and the only verb endings he had to worry about were those for the verb "want."

Figure 8

After his forty hours of self-study, Bernstein hired a foreign student as a tutor and spent a couple of hours a week practicing simple conversations. He didn't spend time with the tutor on drills. He did that on his own time. The evening before he left on a trip he spent three hours with the tutor, speaking only the target language. When he got to the country, he tried to go to restaurants and hotels that were somewhat off the beaten track where English was not commonly spoken.

Bernstein reported considerable success with this method. He used whatever resources were available to him in order to communicate. If words failed, he tried in other ways to get his meanings across. If, for example, he didn't know how to say "I'm finished," he'd simply say "enough" or "no more." He didn't let his lack of knowledge of the language fluster him; he just kept trying until he got his message across. (In other words, he went with his intuition and took risks.)

The point, of course, is that here was a person who used both systematic and intuitive problem-solving strategies in successful combination. His language study program was quite systematic. He had a master plan and fit each language he studied into that plan. But once he was out in the arena where the language must be spoken, he allowed his intuition to take over and didn't worry much about whether he was being systematic or not.

Bernstein's formula might not work ideally for you. You may do better spending less time with the phrase book and tutor and more time getting out there with the natives and surviving. But what Bernstein did show us is that by adopting an effective set of personal strategies and having well-defined goals, you can approach language learning with confidence and with the assurance that you will have at least some measure of success.

Discovering your own strategies for success

By intuitively measuring yourself against each of the cognitive styles that have been discussed in this chapter, you can begin to get a picture of what your own strategies for success might be. In chapter 10 and in the Appendix there are some tests that you can take to determine how you learn, but, for now, your subjective evaluation should be sufficient. The important thing to keep in mind is that self-knowledge is an essential first step toward successful language learning. If you know who you are and what your problem-solving styles are, then you should more easily be able to adapt yourself to your own foreign language learning situation.

Here is a set of principles that have emerged in this chapter:

1. Try to become aware of your own cognitive styles: methods of thinking, taking in information, storing it, and using that information to speak and listen to your foreign language. Remember that these styles are not etched in stone;

they are tendencies that you can modify if necessary. Much of the time you need to utilize both sides of a style continuum, depending on the task at hand.

2. Cognitive styles give rise to specific strategies that you can bring to bear on language learning problems (vocabulary, sound systems, grammar, sentence formation, speaking/ writing styles, etc.). Try to discover some strategies that work especially well for you, even if they don't work that well for someone else.

3. Get your two brain hemispheres to work together. You may need to make your right-brain functions work a little harder than is normally the case in classroom learning.

4. Don't focus too closely, in a field-independent way, on the language you are learning. Look for the all-important forest, not just the trees. Consider backing off from all the words and rules, in a field-sensitive manner, and try to grasp overall meanings of language.

5. Try to be tolerant of the ambiguity that engulfs you as you learn another language. You do need to work at the language, but don't let all the unknowns bother you. Things will probably fall into place in good time.

6. Don't be too preceptive in gathering information about your second language. Be receptive in allowing yourself to absorb as much information as possible even if it doesn't fit your preconceptions about the nature of language.

ANSWERS TO PUZZLES ON PAGE 58

1. J

Not all the five symbols in the pie pieces are alphabetic symbols. The I, V, and X are Roman numerals. Across from each of those numerals are corresponding letters of the alphabet: the first letter, A; the fifth letter, E; and in the blank should appear the tenth letter, J.

2. FLY

The white space in between the black blotches spells the word *fly*. The black is just space in between the letters. We tend to predict that black marks on a white page are relevant. Here they are irrelevant.

3.

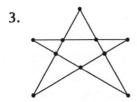

If you draw a star in the traditional way, you will have drawn five lines. A tree at each point and at each intersection of any two lines gives you a total of ten trees in five rows of four trees each.

6

I'm OK—
I Can Do It!

Language learning is physical, mental, and emotional all at once. It involves the development of muscular skills, especially in speech, the intellectual processing of ideas and concepts, and the emotions attendant upon the deep personal engagement demanded by language learning.

Many would agree that of the three classic elements of human existence—the physical, the intellectual, and the emotional—the most fundamental is the emotional, the soul. The emotions are the foundation on which all your learning strategies, techniques, and gimmicks will stand or fall. If you feel good about yourself, have confidence that you can do it, aren't overly anxious, are willing to risk making a fool of yourself from time to time, and have inner motivation to succeed, then the intellectually based techniques discussed in the last two chapters will stand a chance of working. Without that emotional foundation, you are fighting an uphill battle at best.

You may be thinking, "OK, that's no big deal. I'll just decide right here and now that I can do it and that I won't be anxious or inhibited." Well, unfortunately, getting your emotional domain in order is rarely that easy. It takes concentration, effort, and sometimes just plain dogged determination.

What are some of those emotional factors at play in the process of succeeding in a foreign language? Let's look at the principal areas.

Believing in yourself

You don't have to be told that believing in yourself is the key to the attainment of all goals. You've known that for a long time. But as human nature would have it, what we know intellectually doesn't always translate directly into the deeper emotional self that ultimately controls what we do and how we think. Self-doubt has a way of creeping into all the little shadowy corners of our lives and of taking its toll. Scan through the psychology section in a bookstore and you will find dozens of books on the theme of building self-esteem, self-worth, and self-confidence. So, if you ever find yourself with the uneasy feeling of "I can't do it," you are not alone.

The process of second-language learning is so complex and so difficult that self-confidence is a major contributor, if not the keystone, to your success. While it isn't the only factor, all other emotional, intellectual, and physical factors rest upon your ultimate conviction that you can reach the goals you have set. But what if you don't have self-confidence? What if you feel generally good about your mental abilities but feel absolutely rotten when it comes to learning a foreign language? What if you feel okay about language learning in general, but specific *aspects* of learning the language make you feel inadequate? Do any of these questions apply to you? You are not unusual if they do.

Some people, of course, with rather low self-confidence profiles are in need of some ego boosting. If you feel that your general, overall self-confidence is low, this book isn't going to answer that need. Try reading Thomas Harris' *I'm OK—You're OK*,[34] Wayne Dyer's *Pulling Your Own Strings*,[35] or other similar books. For most people, low self-esteem is remedied by finding tasks in which they can succeed and which serve as ego-enhancement experiences. Learning a foreign language, a complex and lengthy process, is an unlikely ego-enhancement task for people with low self-esteem.

Most people have sufficiently high levels of general self-confidence. If, for the most part, you have been successful in attaining goals for yourself, then your general self-confidence level is probably healthy and you should feel modestly confident in your ability to accomplish future goals. There are a few specific areas, however, where many people who are otherwise quite confident of themselves feel inferior to the task.

Figure 9

One of those areas is communicating in a foreign language. Learning a foreign language forces you to become a babbling, bumbling little child, if not a blithering idiot. All of a sudden you are thrust into a situation where your wonderful intellectual capacities, your emotional stability and maturity, and the defensive screens with which you protect yourself in your native language are all left outside the classroom door. You know nothing in the language, or, if you are lucky, you know a few words and stock phrases. You can't express anything of any great importance. And you have no linguistic means for protecting your fragile ego in this strange environment.

In my work with teachers of English as a second language in the United States, I've often been moved by the vulnerability of the foreign students who come to study in this country. Here they are, the cream of the crop back in Japan or Indonesia or Venezuela: the top 5 or 10 percent of their academic peers, competitively screened for study in the U.S., and selected by American institutions. These brave souls end up, in their first semester or so, in our ESL classes designed to help them acquire an English proficiency level that will enable them to compete with their American classmates. Since their proficiency is lower than one would expect, the world's finest scholars are rather abruptly plunked into classes that some people would incorrectly label "bonehead English." Their general self-confidence level somehow remains intact, but their specific self-confidence (how they view themselves just in terms of their English proficiency) is easily shattered. The miracle is that their strong sense of general self-confidence, their belief that they can indeed succeed, carries them along and serves as a reminder that they are not dummies who have somehow lost their intelligence.

You, too, can preserve your sense of self-confidence in the face of the vicissitudes of foreign language learning. Just don't lose sight of yourself as an intelligent, capable, and worthy person. So you are a "babe in the woods" in the language classroom. No problem! Just relax and remember you are in good company. Even if there are some hot shots in the class who talk all the time and make you feel like a fool, you are really okay.

Language ego

From early childhood, our concept of self builds and becomes more and more complex. We learn to protect this delicate organization of values and beliefs as it comes into conflict with other ideas, experiences, and feelings. Gradually, this ego comes to be both understood and expressed through language. In fact, language becomes the most important means by which we understand ourselves, shape our egos, and expose those egos to other people. That is, we give other people glimpses of ourselves through language. It is through language, then, that others come to know us.

The close connection between language and ego has given rise to the concept of *language ego*, a term that refers to the extent to which one's self-concept is inextricably bound up in language. When you talk, you reveal yourself. You reveal what part of the country you are from. You even disclose, often without realizing it, what your socioeconomic level is. The style of speaking you choose (say, informal-conversational vs. formal-rhetorical) is designed to get others to see the side of you that you think is appropriate for the particular occasion. You use language—whether you are speaking, listening, reading, or writing—to your own benefit and to accomplish your own purposes. Usually this happens subconsciously, but surprisingly often you know good and well what you are doing with language. In short, you identify your self-existence with your overall ability to communicate in your native tongue.

Now, think about the repercussions to your ego of learning a second language. Not only does the medium of communication that you are accustomed to using (your native language) suddenly get yanked out from under you, but you also have to build a whole new identity in this new language. Yes, a new language ego, a second identity. As you make progress in the language and it begins to be useful to you, another "you" starts to develop. We will explore this fascinating phenomenon again in the next chapter. For now, let's consider how we protect and guard this ego that's governed by the language we speak.

Shedding your inhibitions

Protecting your ego is so important that it easily becomes an inhibiting factor in language learning. You want very much to avoid exposing your weaknesses, so you stay away from those parts of the language you are not sure of or that might lead to making mistakes. You are terrified of appearing foolish or stupid. So what usually happens? You clam up and only reluctantly venture to say anything at all—and then you stick to the simple and familiar, which involves minimum risk. In short, you play it safe. I have seen so many students shortchange themselves because they were afraid to work at improving the authenticity of their pronunciation. Why? Because they don't want to take the risk of making mistakes or of being thought strange by their peers.

There was once an uninhibited young man from Holland who became very proficient in English. Hans Durbeek reports that as a boy of fourteen he made a regular practice of rehearsing little made-up dialogues in English as he walked to and from school. The other kids thought he was a little crazy, constantly talking to himself, but he persisted and eventually became the best English speaker in his school. Twenty years later, he was almost indistinguishable from a native speaker of English. Granted, his self-rehearsed role plays were not the only contributing factor, but his story illustrates what you can do if you are willing to shed your inhibitions.

In chapter 3 I described the University of Michigan "alcohol experiment." The study concluded that small amounts of alcohol induced a lowering of inhibitions, which gave rise to better success in language learning. Those of us who worked at Michigan at the time had some fun facetiously recommending that the foreign language departments include champagne in what was definitely a beer budget! You, of course, don't need alcohol or drugs to lower your inhibitions and defenses. What you need is a relatively thick skin and fellow learners who respect each other and recognize each other's vulnerability. If you are in a foreign language class now or are about to be in one, try to find a small group of people—a conversation group—with whom to practice your language. If you can coax or hire someone proficient in the language to serve as a tutor, so much the better. But at least work on the principle that a small group of people is much less inhibiting than a classroom full. Even then, when you are in the classroom, try to discard your inhibitions. Remember that you are all in this together, so take the plunge and make a fool of yourself with joy and confidence.

Risk taking

A consideration of self-confidence and inhibition would hardly be complete without mention of the notion of risk taking. We have already seen (chapter 5) how second-language learning involves gambling, guessing, and acting on hunches. In other words, you have to be able to risk being wrong. That can be scary.

Make no mistake about it, your fears are real. You aren't imagining the reproaches from the teacher, the smirks from classmates, or the blank look of a listener when you have failed to communicate. Those things all happen in a foreign language class. Blank looks and rebuffs also happen outside the classroom. In the face of these verbal and nonverbal onslaughts to your ego, you have to be willing to put forth again and again, to keep risking the possibility that you will fail.

One time a group of students from a high school French club happened to knock on my door to solicit support for their activities. As soon as I learned they were from the French club I broke into my own somewhat imperfect French, *"Ah, c'est très bien, alors. Vous parlez français! S'il vous plait, entrez...nous pouvons parler en français un petit peu?"* Upon hearing what to their ears was a barrage of French, they looked at each other in embarrassment, then looked back at me, and quickly—in English—thanked me for my interest and left. They weren't about to reveal that French 1A in the local high school had in no way prepared them to enter into even the most rudimentary conversation. The risk in attempting it would have been too great.

But your risks can be calculated. Research studies have shown that people can be categorized on a scale from high to low risk takers. High risk takers are often wild and frivolous in their attempts. On the other side (where most of us are), low risk takers are too protective, and while their percentage of guesses may be better, their rate of progress is likely to be much slower. Nothing ventured, nothing gained.

But this same research also shows that those who fall somewhere in between high and low risk-taking styles are usually more successful in overall learning. The same is true of language learning. Your goal, then, should be to develop a pattern of moderate risk taking such that you can play the odds. You can afford to be a little audacious, but by the same token don't always be the one to blurt out an answer or to engage in incessant fractured blather. Hold back enough to give yourself time to figure out when it is best to speak or to assume you have interpreted something correctly or to draw a conclusion about how the language works. Try to become a calculated risk taker. Good language learners are willing and relatively accurate guessers.

Foreign language anxiety

The headline in an Ann Arbor newspaper some years back read, "Doing math is an emotional experience." The article went on to deal with a common ailment: math anxiety. One person testified, "If you want to see me panic, all you have to say is, 'If two men dig a ditch in one hour....'" Another said, "When I see figures, I immediately feel I can't do it. Take them away." And still another confessed, "I just panic, block, freeze up."[36]

Do you have foreign language anxiety? The symptoms aren't much different: feelings of intimidation and inadequacy over the prospect of learning a foreign language. Why all this anxiety? Sometimes the cause is methods of instruction that are commonly used in classrooms. You are forced to learn grammar, memorize dialogues and vocabulary, translate from one language to the other, and write out vapid little exercises. And throughout this maze of intellectual activity, you feel forced into a defensive posture by the demand that you recite correctly when the teacher calls on you.

You can avoid some of this anxiety by using numerous strategies that have been suggested in this book. Decide for yourself to chart your own course. Then you won't be confined only to what the teacher dictates. Instead of being a victim, you start to pull your own strings a bit. This alone will relieve a great deal of the defensive, classroom-oriented anxiety that scares off all too many potentially successful learners.

But anxiety doesn't just come from the classroom. It also comes from deep within. Some of us find foreign languages difficult because we are conditioned to believe that languages are difficult. People say, "French was a bear of a course," "I hated German, it was super difficult," "Don't take a foreign language if you can help it." The statistics cited in the first chapter of this book—showing the miserable performance of Americans in foreign languages—are in themselves enough to generate negative thinking on your part. Don't let these self-fulfilling prophecies take their course. Your best bet is to ignore the bad press. Don't let the failures of others (for reasons that probably don't apply to you at all) convince you beforehand that you are not going to make it.

Figure 10

A final, more positive thought about anxiety. Educational research shows that a small amount of anxiety can actually be beneficial to learning. If you have ever given a public speech, acted in a play, or played team sports, you know the feeling of butterflies in your stomach that you get beforehand. As long as those butterflies don't make you fall completely flat on your face, they may be an outward sign of facilitative anxiety: a level of tension within you, caused by a little surge of adrenaline, that stimulates you and spurs your determination to do well. This mild level of facilitative anxiety is therefore a positive sign.

Hamming it up in the foreign language

Do you enjoy big parties with lots of people? Do you usually take the initiative in a conversation? Do you talk with strangers easily? If so, you may be an extrovert, and you will probably approach a foreign language differently from an introvert, who is less comfortable interacting with lots of people and who enjoys solitude. Depending on where you fall on the continuum, you will bring different abilities and needs to the task of learning a foreign language.

Actually, extroversion is a widely misunderstood term. Many of us have been led to think that an extrovert is always the life of a party, the first to raise a hand in the classroom, loud, and maybe even bordering on obnoxious. But those behaviors could come from an introvert whose defenses are high. Extroversion, in its technical definition, is the need (and ability) to receive ego gratification and a sense of wholeness from other people. Introversion is the need and ability to derive this sense of self-esteem from within oneself. Because a good many extroverts exhibit gregarious behavior, our society has come to value extroversion. Even in the classroom, those who raise their hands often and who participate willingly and frequently are highly valued and rewarded by teachers. Quiet, reserved behavior is sometimes viewed as passive. In other cultures, the opposite behavior is valued: the quiet, reserved student is considered smart and is rewarded for his or her good behavior.

In reality, extroversion isn't always expressed in stereotypically loud or assertive behavior. Extroverts simply need others as a mirror to see themselves. They derive their sense of happiness and fulfillment from being with and receiving affirmation from other people. To receive such affirmation you don't always need to give a lot of yourself; you can just "be there."

On the other side of the coin, introversion is too often maligned in our culture. Introverts are simply able to find affirmation within themselves. There is, in fact, an inner strength implied in introversion that isn't often recognized. So if someone ever says, "You're a real introvert, aren't you?" you might want to take it as a compliment.

How do these ideas help you find your pathway to foreign language success? First, try to understand yourself in terms of an introversion/extroversion continuum. In the Appendix, one of the diagnostic tests measures extroversion and introversion. When you get to chapter 10, where you are directed to take that test, you will find out where you lie on that continuum, and then you can tackle your language learning accordingly.

If you are on the extroverted side, capitalize on your ability to derive fulfillment from being with others. Use the foreign language as much as possible as a vehicle for achieving that fulfillment. In the classroom, go ahead and ham it up a little bit.

If you are on the introverted side of the continuum, reaching out to others, even quietly, may require a little concentrated effort on your part. But the effort is well worth making. Your ability to keep to yourself may work against you in learning a foreign language, even though it will work for you when you study on your own. Understanding and mastering the system of the new language may also sometimes be a little easier for the introvert. But the ability to use language for communication is best attained in the arena of communal interaction, and the sooner you stick your neck out and get yourself into the fray, the better.

The language game

We can hardly consider the emotional side of language learning without a look at the "game" of language. Games of the sort we are talking about here involve some level of intellectual activity, but without an emotional basis, they quickly lose their gamelike quality.

Twenty-seven years ago Eric Berne's bestseller, *Games People Play*, introduced the American public to the gamelike quality of our relationships with other people. "Most people, in most of their family and business relationships, are constantly playing games with each other. What's more, they are striving—often unconsciously—for an emotional 'payoff' which is startlingly different from what they might rationally expect to get from winning or losing their game."[37] Berne cautions that games are not necessarily fun, nor do we play all of them in a literal sense. Nevertheless, we immerse ourselves in game playing every day.

Berne identified two distinguishing qualities of games: (1) there are always ulterior motives or hidden reasons for the actions taken, and (2) there is always a payoff—someone wins. Every game, according to Berne, is basically dishonest and its outcome normally provides someone with a more or less dramatic reward. Think about football or chess, for example. Their ulterior nature is seen in hidden strategies, setting up for a running play, for instance, while actually planning a pass play, or sacrificing a knight to divert the attention of your opponent while you close in for checkmate. The payoff is the "win," the ecstasy of victory.

Berne said human communication games share the same qualities. You flirt in a sexual game, hiding your inner thoughts and intentions, anticipating the return of similar sexual messages. Or when you desperately need a raise, you butter up the boss but stop just short of gushing. Your payoff is the attention you get and, of course, the raise. Everyone plays games, and language is the vehicle for these games. Think about them: students' games, teachers' games, lovers' games, spouses' games, children's games, parents' games, and on and on.

Learning a foreign language means learning not just the words and sentences and cultural connotations of the language, but learning how to play life games in the language too. What a task! It's hard enough to play all these games in our own language. How can you, as a learner, handle such complexity?

First of all, you will be better off if, at the beginning, you don't worry about complex, language-based game playing. Instead, play the simple games that are more or less universal. Suppose you are in a foreign country and you know three words in the language. The people aren't friendly and you desperately need a taxi. Play the same game you would play in New York, nonverbally. Who knows, it might work. Or say you are in Japan and everybody is bowing and smiling at you, and you can't stand it. Well, play the game: bow back, smile a lot, and your payoff will be to get what you need when you need it.

Games learners play

The gaming metaphor doesn't just apply to principles of human communication. Another useful application of gaming is to actually make your own games of the language learning experience. Have you ever considered what a wonderful game language learning is? You can approach language learning as you would a game of poker or tennis or whatever your favorite game is. There are two phases to this game:

getting the language that's "out there" channeled into your brain, and then using it productively to accomplish some end. The ulterior part (although it doesn't have to be that big a secret) is the set of strategies you adopt to take in the words, sentences, rules or whatever, along with the techniques you use to facilitate getting the language into the ears and eyes of others. The payoff—the actual use of language in real-life contexts—can be dramatic as you surprise yourself with how much you can accomplish.

When I first went to Japan, I spent some time with a phrase book learning useful phrases à la Leonard Bernstein. With my phonetics training and language background, it didn't take much effort for me to gain a fairly authentic pronunciation of a dozen stock phrases. My game was to use the phrases in Japan, pretending I knew Japanese. I said a few words or phrases and then thanked people profusely, which endeared me to them. The payoff came numerous times when I learned the price of something, got the food I had ordered, and found places—including bathrooms—for which I had asked directions.

My game didn't always pay off, especially when the Japanese would start jabbering back at me in language I couldn't possibly decipher, at which point I had to find a way either to graciously end the little conversation or simply confess that I couldn't understand. In a sense they called my bluff. But I had fun and was much happier playing the game than I would have been in safe enclaves of fellow American tourists protected by cadres of translating tour guides.

Without going into detail, here are some other possible language games you can play:

- The music game. Set words, phrases, and/or sentences to a familiar tune and sing it. You'd be surprised how music etches certain strings of language into the brain. Sing these sentences back to yourself or use snatches of measures as you try to communicate.
- The mnemonics game. Make associations between, say, noun or verb endings and a little sentence in English.
- The kazoo game. In studying a language (like Chinese) where intonation makes a big difference in meaning, practice speaking

through a kazoo; you will hear only the tones and be able to discern the accuracy of your intonation.
- The noun-verb game. Try speaking a language by using only nouns and verbs and don't worry about inflections. You may be surprised at the payoff.
- The visualization game. Visualize yourself speaking the language fluently and interacting with people. Then when you are actually in such a situation, you will, in a sense, have "been there" before.

Virtually every strategy or gimmick that has been mentioned so far in this book can become a game. The difference between games and dead-serious ritual is that you can take a lighthearted perspective. Some games are won, some are lost. That's life, and that's okay.

Motivation

Anyone can easily argue that motivation is the key to all learning and all successes. If you are motivated, you'll do it. Give yourself enough of a reason or reward for something, and you are a sure bet. Okay, but that's an oversimplification. What, after all, is motivation? And how do you create and maintain it?

A thorough answer to these questions ultimately leads us back to basic human needs, even to those as fundamental as survival needs like air, water, and food, which are the foundation tier of Maslow's[38] "pyramid," or hierarchy of needs. The next layers consist of needs for safety, order, and belonging. Further up the pyramid we find such needs as achievement, mastery, and self-esteem. Finally, at the peak is *self-actualization* as we ultimately become all that we are capable of becoming. All these basics are components of our needs system from which we derive motivation, that is, the *anticipation of fulfilling perceived needs.*

Here is a list of needs that are particularly crucial to developing and maintaining the motivation to keep pressing on in a foreign language:

1. The need for *exploration*, for seeing "the other side of the mountain," for probing the unknown
2. The need for *manipulation,* for causing change in the environment and in other people
3. The need for *activity*, for movement and exercise, both physical and mental
4. The need for *stimulation*, for rewards and pleasure from others, from the environment, or simply from ideas, thoughts, and feelings
5. The need for *knowledge*, for figuring out and conceptualizing the world around us, for resolving contradictions and solving problems
6. The need for *ego enhancement*, for feeling accepted, appreciated, and valued by other people

Motivation is the anticipation of the satisfaction of needs. We do something because we expect certain needs within us to be satisfied. A child who is motivated to learn to read anticipates that his or her needs for exploration, stimulation, and knowledge—among others—will be met. Failure to learn to read may be due in part to being unable to anticipate sufficient rewards.

Motivation to learn a foreign language will increase as you perceive more and more deeply that some needs are going to be met. Learning a foreign language can help you meet these needs by enabling you to

1. *explore* new places, new cultures, new people;
2. *accomplish new goals* in your life, or otherwise manipulate your environment;
3. engage in *mental activity* as you immerse yourself in this new intellectual enterprise;
4. *gain incentive* through the new vistas and new payoffs as the language actually begins to work for you;
5. acquire new *knowledge* of ways of expressing yourself, or of the complexities of the system of the language; and
6. experience *ego enhancement* as you discover not only that you can indeed learn another language but also that others praise and admire you for it.

One of the major reasons that Americans are somewhat tongue-tied is that we don't easily perceive motives for language learning. We are too insular and rely for communication on the growing millions of people on earth who have learned English. Fortunately, some of these conditions and impressions are changing as travel becomes easier and as more people in this country maintain the use of their non-English native languages. (The United States is now the fourth largest Spanish-speaking country in the world.) If we want to, we can find people right here in this country with whom we can speak a foreign language.

There are other motives for second-language learning that you might make your own. In chapter 1 we learned that more and more jobs are requiring foreign language proficiency. Corporations in this country are beginning to realize that communication is a two-way street and we had better learn some of those languages "out there" and not just wait for "them" to learn English. Furthermore, foreign languages act as a vehicle for understanding other peoples and appreciating the rich cultural diversity of our planet. Is there anyone who doesn't enjoy this panorama of people, nations, races, literatures, and world views? A foreign language is a passport to those new worlds.

I'm OK—I can do it!

Having read this chapter, you should now be able to add a few more pieces to the mastery-of-a-foreign-language puzzle. Some of the most important pieces are these:

1. Believe in yourself. You don't have to be a genius to master a foreign language.
2. Although as a foreign language learner, you are in a vulnerable situation and may feel defenseless, your healthy, overall self-confidence will see you through.
3. Try to shed your natural inhibitions about behaving in ways that you think make you look foolish. Go ahead and jump

right in; and if you make a fool of yourself in the process, just laugh about it. It doesn't really hurt.

4. Take some calculated risks. If you always play it safe, you will never get anywhere at all.

5. No doubt you will feel some anxiety as you take those risks, but that's okay. A certain amount of anxiety can be beneficial.

6. Try to maintain and/or develop your extroverted tendencies; they will help you to be more other-oriented as you communicate in the foreign language.

7. Language is used to play some of life's more intricate games, but don't worry about that at the beginning. Just make language learning itself a set of little games.

8. There are a number of deep-seated needs within us that can be tapped as motives for learning a foreign language. If you don't already feel strongly motivated, try to identify how learning a language will meet these needs.

7

Joining
the Language Club

Not long ago, Washington columnist and radio commentator Rick
Horowitz[39] printed the following column in a number of newspapers
across the country.

POLITICS TO THE MAX

Like, I don't even know where to start, you know? Melissa and I are
at the mall the other day, you know, looking at these awesome
bracelets, and here comes Krissie, and she goes, "It passed! It passed!"
Like, you know, we know what she's talking about.

So then Melissa goes to Krissie, "Get a grip, girl!" because, you
know, she was just freaking out, totally. "What passed?" We figure,
you know, some dude went by on a truly tubular set of wheels or
something. You know Krissie—any twerp with an engine and she's
charred.

So anyway, Melissa goes, "What passed?" and Krissie goes, "The
referendum!" And I look at Melissa and Melissa looks at me, and we

both, like, crack up, you know? And we go, "Wow! Pretty awesome, Krissie"—you know, like we're serious—"What referendum?"

So Krissie goes, "The English language referendum! They voted for it!" and people all over the mall start to look at us, and it's a total face, I swear, because they probably think I pay attention to politics—barf me out! So we finally drag Krissie off to some corner—she can be such a hosehead sometimes—and cool her out.

So then she tells us about this referendum that was on the California ballot to make English the official language. I'm wrapped about the whole thing—like, who cares, you know? But Melissa, she says her father was cranking his gums about it the other night, about how there are all these Mexicans all over the place now and they talked so that you can't even understand them, you know, and now they want the government to, like, talk to them in Mexican or something. The same with the Chinese, he says.

I go to Melissa, "Take off!" because even I know there's no way the government's going to talk Chinese. The letters they use—I bought this sweatshirt one time, and, like, it had letters on it in Chinese or something. It was totally rad, you know, but you couldn't even read it.

Then Krissie gets truly edged. "Will you listen to me?!" she goes. "This is gnarly!" And then she says the referendum means, like, the Mexicans and everybody will have to learn English if they want to get along with everybody else.

So I go, "You're lensed to the max, Krissie. Who cares about some grody referendum?"

Krissie looks at me like I'm a total gel, you know. Then she goes, "What language do you speak, Tamara?"

I go, "English."

Then she goes, "And what's California's official language going to be?"

And I go, "English."

Then she goes, "And who speaks 'official languages'?"

And I go, "Politicians."

"Who else?"

"Policemen?"

"And who else?"

"TEACHERS?"

She goes, "Fer sure."

"Gag me with a spoon! You mean, every one of those geeks at

school will be, you know, talking just the way we do? That's so gross! I'm like totally ruined!"

Then Krissie goes, "Still think I'm lensed?" And she walks right out of the mall.

So now me and Melissa are thinking of learning Chinese. Bummer.

Conversations like these happen across the country and around the world every day: conversations in which a person's spoken language is a sign of membership in what Frank Smith[40] has called the "spoken language club." Think about what most clubs are like. There is an air of exclusivity about them. Those who belong and those who don't are clearly defined, and often those who are "in" have ways—through dress, money, job, and even personality—of seeing to it that those who are "out" are kept out. There are conventional forms for maintaining membership. You have to follow rules, written and unwritten, to maintain your status. Sometimes the unwritten, covert rules are more important than the outward, formal ones. You bind yourself to other club members by keeping the rules and thereby create a feeling of solidarity and of belonging.

Look again at Horowitz' vignette. Tamara and Melissa are quite obviously speaking a language that identifies them as members of that most enigmatic of all clubs, the teenage "adults barf me out" club. One of the principal ways they define themselves is through the language they use to communicate. Horowitz has painted a marvelous, if a bit stereotypical, picture of the exclusivity of this club and how its members maintain their status, even to the ironic little twist at the end where the speaker is aghast at the thought of enlarging that membership.

On my first visit to Japan I was amused by the use of English words and letters on T-shirts, notebooks, and other personal items. Most of these words and/or letters have no intrinsic meaning. They are simply emblems identified as English, through which the value of the item is mysteriously increased. A whole line of school supplies carries the label "Hello Kitty." The school kids love it. I asked one university student, who was wearing a sweatshirt with "The Nature University" printed on it, where that university was. "Oh," she answered with a little titter, "is just words, no such place exist."

In Japan English words symbolize a club of sorts: the club of those who know—or think they know, or even who would like to know—English. That's an important club to belong to. Even though English is a required subject for six years of secondary school, only a tiny fraction of high school graduates in Japan actually learn to communicate in English. Even those who major in English in college find the goal of speaking English, if not writing it, an elusive one. English symbolizes an intellectual status of sorts, a club to which few can belong. If you wear a T-shirt or carry a notebook with English words on them, you gain the appearance of belonging to an exclusive club.

When you learn a second language, you join a language club. As you become proficient in the language, you accumulate merit points that can ultimately admit you to the group of speakers of that language. Now, in some cases you may find that current members will, either intentionally or inadvertently, rule you out as a possible initiate in the club. Sometimes those lifetime members are justified in their exclusivity. When I was in Naples a few years ago, I had to travel on my own to Rome by train. Determined to make my phrase-book Italian work, as I got my ticket I asked (in my best Italian accent) *"Dove il treno per Roma?"* The station agent replied, in perfect English, "Down that hallway, fifth track on your left." There was no way I was going to be able to join his Italian language club. I willingly let him join my English club.

At times you may be the object of some prejudice on the part of club members. They might think you talk funny, seem too loud or too quiet, don't look quite right, or don't smell right. You will need to be prepared to meet such biases along the way. If your skin is thick enough, you should be able to survive a few rebuffs without permanent damage.

More often, however, your efforts will be openly welcomed and taken as a compliment to the club members' culture, language, or country. If you stick with it, you will find many who will reward you by opening the club doors.

You are what you speak

It was Frank Smith[41] again who remarked that perhaps one of the most offensive things you can say to someone is, "I don't like the

Figure 11

way you talk." People can make fun of your clothing, your hairstyle, your intelligence, or even your ancestry, but if they ridicule the way you talk, the hurt is deep and lasting. Why? Because you can't hide the way you talk. You can change clothes and hairstyle, deceive people about intelligence, and finesse the ancestry question, but your verbal behavior is so up front and undisguisable and so deeply a part of you that the minute you open your mouth you are exposed and vulnerable. Speech is the emblem of who you are.

In the previous chapter the concept of "language ego" was introduced. It refers to the way in which your self-concept and sense of self-esteem are intertwined with language and the degree to which, in language transactions, your ego is exposed. As you grow mentally and emotionally during childhood, you slowly develop an individual identity. Integral to this identity is the language you speak. Indeed, it has been argued that language is the primary means of defining and expressing human identity.

As you increase your proficiency in a second language, you will inevitably begin to take on a second identity. If you have already learned a foreign language and can use it in daily situations, you know that you are a slightly different "you" when speaking it. As a child growing up in what was then the Belgian Congo (now Zaire), I had a very clear conception of myself as a different person when I was conversing with my African friends. I was not African; I could never be African. But the identity that interacted with Africans in Kikongo was more Africanized than the identity I perceived when I was with my parents and other Americans.

The prospect of becoming fluent in a second language takes on a pervasive psychological nature. The self that you have grown comfortable with is suddenly faced with an additional self: a foreign language self that thinks, feels, and acts differently. One scholar likened this acquisition of a second identity to schizophrenia. You can well imagine how two personas develop within you as you become bilingual.

As you begin to take on that new persona, you also begin to take on the culture of that language, even if you never actually set foot in the culture. Language and culture are inextricably bound together. Culture is the set of conventions and rules for operating within the language club. On the surface you may learn words, apply rules of grammar, and practice pronunciation and all those other necessary aspects of language learning. But beneath that surface is your ultimate purpose: to communicate with those who use the language. People don't exist in a vacuum any more than club members exist without a club. They are a part of some framework: a family, a community, a country, a set of traditions, a storehouse of knowledge, a way of looking at the universe. In short, every person is part of a culture, and everyone uses a language to express that culture. Whenever we open our mouths to speak, we are transmitting not just language but complex cultural messages as well.

Look at the conversation at the beginning of this chapter again and consider how hard it would be for a person who was learning English as a second language to understand it. The next time you listen to a comedian, imagine yourself trying to listen to the humor with little or no American cultural knowledge. Yakov Smirnoff once did a beer commercial where he said, "In America, you can always find a party. In Russia the party always finds you!" Without some cultural knowledge, the humor of the statement escapes you.

The point is that language learning goes far beyond merely learning words, rules, phrases, and linguistic systems. It means learning a new culture and taking on a second cultural identity—a second mode of thinking, feeling, and acting. Eventually, you will find that you actually think differently when you use the second language and you will experience the feeling that "you are what you speak." And here is one of the greatest joys of language learning—participating in, and celebrating, human diversity.

Using and misusing stereotypes

Culture learning is a relatively complicated process, and it therefore usually begins with oversimplification and stereotyping.

Think about the stereotypes that you, as an American, might have regarding people from other cultures. The British are reserved, overly polite, thrifty, precise with language, and they drink tea at four o'clock. Italians are passionate, demonstrative, and they drink red wine with pasta. Germans are stubborn, industrious, methodical, and they drink beer every night. Asians are reserved, wise, cunning, inscrutable, and they, too, drink tea. On the other hand, how do these other cultures perceive Americans? We are rich, informal if not impolite, materialistic, and too friendly. We drive large cars, live in the suburbs, and eat at fast food restaurants. Our political leaders like to be seen chopping wood or relaxing in jeans and tennis shoes.

François Lierres, writing in a Paris magazine, once gave some tongue-in-cheek advice to French people on how to get along with Americans. "They are the Vikings of the world economy, descending upon it in their jets as the Vikings once did in their *drakars*. They have money, technology, and nerve. We would be wise to get acquainted with them."[42] He went on to offer some "dos" and "don'ts." Among the dos: Greet them, but after you have been introduced once, don't shake hands, merely emit a cluck of joy— "hi!" Speak without emotion, with self-assurance, giving the impression you have a command of the subject even if you haven't. Check the collar of your jacket—nothing is uglier in the eyes of an American than dandruff. Radiate congeniality and show a good disposition—a big smile and a warm expression are essential. Learn how to play golf. Then, among the don'ts: Don't tamper with your accent—Maurice Chevalier was well liked in America. And don't allow the slightest smell of perspiration to reach the easily offended nostrils of your American friends.

Not all of our penchant for stereotyping is bad. Some notions are derived from legitimate cultural characteristics that we need to be aware of. We need to understand that the French really *are* different from Americans in important ways, and we had better understand those differences before we do business with them or invite them to our homes for dinner.

Stereotypes have a way of broadly defining club membership. If you are careful not to attend just to negative stereotypes, then positive stereotypes can help to balance the picture for you. Those positives can also help you understand that all stereotyping arises out of our particular worldview. Traits are only relative to the traits of another culture. So, Latin Americans are perceived as loud simply because we perceive them as louder than Americans. Americans, on the other hand, seem loud to Japanese.

Look beyond the general characteristics of the people whose language you are learning. Recognize that every person is unique and that the people you talk with will in some way violate the stereotypes. After all, even carefully defined and measured cultural characteristics are only statistical norms from which individuals vary greatly. So, don't expect everyone you meet to fall into stereotypical patterns. After all, you don't fall into all of the American stereotypes.

Walking in their shoes

Stereotyping usually implies a particular attitude on your part toward the culture. And attitudes toward a culture spill over into your feelings about the language itself. If for some reason you dislike, say, Italians, you may also have a subtle dislike of the Italian language. Obviously, your motivation to learn such a language is going to be adversely affected.

I once came across a startling example of a negative bias that stemmed from a stereotype. It appeared in a 1940 encyclopedia in a description of Chinese literature. Here's an excerpt:

> The Chinese language is monosyllabic and uninflectional...with a language so incapable of variation, a literature cannot be produced which possesses the qualities we look for and admire in literary works. Elegance, variety, beauty of imagery—these must all be lacking. A monotonous and wearisome language must give rise to a forced and formal literature lacking in originality and interesting in its subject matter only. Moreover, a conservative people...profoundly reverencing all that is old and formal, and hating innovation, must leave the impress of its own character upon its literature.[43]

If you took these claims to heart, would you want to learn Chinese?

In joining the language club, it is important, as it is in joining any club, that you value the association with the other members. You have to feel that they are interesting, intelligent, and worth mingling with and getting to know. If you are biased against, say, Germans, you'd best leave your biases at the door when you enter the German language club. Actually, most people find that little biases and stereotypes they may have at the outset are easily dispelled as they interact in the foreign language with real live people. Talking with people in their language is a great equalizer.

The key to developing positive attitudes is empathy—the ability to put yourself in someone else's shoes. But developing cultural empathy is easier said than done. Each one of us is so thoroughly conditioned by our own culture and our identities are so entwined with it that projecting ourselves into a foreign culture is no simple task. Nevertheless, it's essential to make the effort.

At the same time, the empathy you develop for the other culture shouldn't be allowed to threaten your own cultural identity. Just because you understand other cultures doesn't mean you close out membership in your native language club. In fact, empathy, as the term is used by therapists and counselors, implies a modicum of detachment along with understanding. Just as a good counselor understands clients without taking on their woes and tribulations, so you can empathize with people of another culture without necessarily assimilating into it and/or losing your primary cultural identity.

The well-known anthropologist, Margaret Mead, had to learn a number of languages in order to carry out her field research. She reported, on one occasion, that she was a "seat of the pants" learner who capitalized on her empathetic skills. In an interview she remarked:

> I am not a good mimic and I have worked now in many different cultures. I am a very poor speaker of any language, but I always know whose pig is dead, and when I work in the native society, I know what people are talking about and I treat it seriously and I respect them, and this in itself establishes a great deal more rapport, very often, than the "correct accent." I have worked with other field workers who were far, far better linguists than I, and the natives kept on saying those people couldn't speak the language, although they said *I* could! Now, if you had a recording of me it would be proof positive I couldn't, but nobody knew it![44]

Margaret Mead felt that rapport and shared knowledge and experience were the most important factors in learning a language. If you know the people, empathize with them, and try to understand them fully, then language will follow.

Haragei

Achieving empathy with another culture is sometimes made difficult by subtle contrasts. A poignant example of contrasting cultural communication patterns is the Japanese concept of what is known as *haragei*. In a speech to language teachers in Japan, newspaper columnist Michihiro Matsumoto[45] illustrated haragei with an anecdote.

> Five famous Jewish intellectuals were up in heaven discussing the essence of life. Moses said, "The essence of life is in your head." Jesus Christ said, "No, the essence of life is in the heart." Then Karl Marx said, "You're both wrong. The most important thing in life is the stomach—you've got to keep it fed." Sigmund Freud said, "Gentlemen, you're all wrong. The most important thing is further below the belt." And Albert Einstein said, "You're all off the mark. Everything is relative." A Japanese intellectual who overheard the conversation just kept silent, with an enigmatic smile on his face, nodding assent to each remark. So Moses asked the Japanese, "What's your view?" The Japanese responded, "What you all feel is what I feel." "But whose view, specifically?" asked Freud. "Well," said the Japanese, "if I think in my head, Einstein's. But I don't think in my head; I think in my *hara* (abdomen). Thinking in my head gives rise to yes or no. The essence of life is not yes or no, but yes *and* no, because yes means no and no means yes."

Matsumoto went on to explain how "hara-thinking," or haragei, is the essence of Japanese culture. Haragei is the product of an agrarian culture where farmers pull together to "group think," "group feel," or "group behave" for a mutually shared goal. Individualism is the antithesis of haragei. Matsumoto explained that Japanese society is like *natto*, a fermented soybean cake. If you pluck at a natto cake, you discover that the beans are held together by a sticky, tasteless paste. In Japan the sticky paste that binds individuals together is made up of the social connections of family, group, company, financial world, and government. All are interlinked. Harmony and empathy are ultimate values.

Haragei-ists refuse to be pinned down, or to answer yes or no, which would dichotomize and polarize. Harmony is promoted by diminishing, not increasing, debate. Matsumoto pointed out that America is a "why-because" culture where debate, definition, distinction, and delineation are encouraged. Japanese prefer the vague, imprecise, elusive, and unspecified. Linguistic illustrations are numerous. The word *wakarimashita*, usually translated as "I understand," can, when spoken by a Japanese, mean "I understand," "I agree," "I hear you," "Forget it," or "The case is closed."

It is this characteristic of their communication that leads us to label Japanese as inscrutable—we can never seem to figure out what they really think. But Matsumoto pointed out that haragei is a very positive concept for the Japanese. It allows listeners to fill in the blanks, to provide their own interpretations, and to come to an understanding of how they can agree, rather than disagree, with each other.

I once spent a week in Japan trying to negotiate a faculty exchange contract with a Japanese university. I became increasingly frustrated as the week wore on with what seemed to be oblique responses to my proposals, punctuated by bows and nods of the head that were impossible to decipher. I could never get a clear yes or no from my negotiators. Every suggestion was received with a polite "wakarimashita," which to my Western mind meant "I understand." Only later did I discover that it probably meant something on the order of "forget it." Second-language learning is a process of empathetically reaching out and looking at the universe in another way.

Culture shock

If you doubt that you will ever have the chance to live abroad for an extended time, you may wonder if a consideration of culture shock is relevant. In some ways it may not be. On the other hand, culture shock is only a specialized word for a common psychological experience that can occur anywhere—even within your own country. I experienced culture shock when I moved from Ann Arbor, Michigan, to Champaign-Urbana, Illinois. And in relatively short visits to foreign countries, people have reported various symptoms of culture shock. It is therefore useful to know something about it.

For people who move to another country—immigrants, long-term residents—language learning and culture learning interact in rather curious ways. After an early stage of euphoria, things in the new country begin to get to you. The food is too spicy; the people are indifferent; you can't find what you want in the stores; your house is too cold; transportation systems don't work; and on and on. The result is persistent feelings of mild depression which eventually become what is known as culture shock, a stage in which just about everything that is different in the new country is annoying.

Meanwhile, your language learning has probably gone through parallel stages. At first you are pleasantly surprised that you can actually communicate with the natives a bit. With a few phrases here and some body language there, you feel pretty good about yourself. But as time wears on, you recognize your deficiencies and are painfully aware of how little your classroom language learning has prepared you for real-life interaction. You become irritated and frustrated when progress is slow. Your linguistic frustration combines with culture shock to feed your depression, and soon you are ready to pack your bags and go home.

Figure 12

Ironically, research has found that it is just at this point that you reach a critical stage in which you can turn things around. The cultural stress and language distress you feel is normal and, more important, the solution to your stress is right around the corner. If you resist packing your bags and hang in there, you will be in an optimal state of motivation both to develop your skills in cross-cultural adjustment and to learn the language. You will never have felt before then as much need to find a way to survive in the country. That need can be a trigger to renewed efforts to increase your linguistic skills as a means of surviving. Culture shock can thus become the ultimate spur to successful language learning. Most people who manage at this point to redouble their language learning efforts also end up successfully coping with culture shock.

Even if you don't spend a long time living in the country—where cultural factors play such an intrusive role—you still have miniature culture shock experiences during shorter-term visits. You may feel elated during the first few days of your summer trip abroad. But after two weeks of small hotel rooms, strange bathroom fixtures, congested streets, pestering street vendors, and missed train connections, you might feel just a touch of culture stress and linguistic frustration. Hang in there. You only have a temporary associate membership in their club, but they will eventually let you into their rituals if you show interest and empathy—even if only to get your money.

Language club rules in short

There are rules and conventions that must be adhered to in any club. The language club has its own rules (discussed in this chapter), which, in brief look something like this:

1. Speech is the emblem of your identify. When you talk with others, you are letting them know who you are, and vice versa. Emulate others' speech and you will get into the club more easily.

2. Learning a foreign language involves taking on a second identity, a different "you" that may be at odds with your native-language self. Don't be afraid to recognize that new identity. Try to become comfortable with it.

3. Language and culture are so intricately woven together that second-language learning is also second-culture learning. Learn everything you can about the new culture.

4. Beware of stereotypes. While they may provide useful generalizations about another culture, they often don't apply to the particular people you come into contact with.

5. Try to develop a positive attitude toward the people whose language you are learning. Appreciate them and their worldview. Try walking around in their shoes.

6. Sometimes learning another language calls for a completely different way of *thinking.* In Japanese, for example, haragei constitutes a way of thinking and communicating that is entirely different from the Western or American way. Try to figure out how to think in your foreign language.

7. If you go to live in another culture, remember that feelings of culture stress and even culture shock are natural, normal experiences. You can convert your distress into a strong motivator for learning.

8

Making Your Mistakes Work for You

One day in the morning
It was hot continue one month ago.
Look at everywhere with sad.
The leaves fell down when the wind blow.
On the floor full of leaves,
Side by side everywhere.
Anything was confusion.
Look like somebody was to trouble
By poorness of mankind.

e. e. cummings? Emily Dickinson? No, this little poem was written by a university student from Japan who was learning English in the United States. He was asked to write a simple paragraph describing a photograph that depicted a park after a violent summer windstorm. The only change I have made is to transform his paragraph structure into lines of verse.

This creation came from a person who was relatively new at the business of writing the English language. It has grammar errors and incomplete sentences. Some writing teachers would fill such a paragraph with red ink. It contains a number of typical errors made by people learning English as a second language. Nevertheless, the verse evokes feeling and imagery. It reminds one of those playful e. e. cummings pieces.

We have been conditioned through our schooling to consider errors as negative. Errors have come to signify falling short of goals, if not outright failure. Perfection is thought of as errorlessness. Some methods of teaching a foreign language even advocate the complete avoidance of errors. Nelson Brooks once said of the language learning process, "One does not learn by making mistakes, but rather by giving the right response."[46] The absurdity of such a claim is easily seen if you just think of a skill you currently have—playing a sport, solving math problems, using a computer, playing a musical instrument. Then consider the implications of suggesting that the skill might have been acquired without ever going through a process of trial and error. Methods of language teaching that follow such maxims would never succeed in teaching people to communicate in real-life situations.

We learned in earlier chapters that children make mistakes all the time as they develop both first- and second-language skills. Children learning English as a native language will come up with utterances like, "Want milk," "I catched the ball," and "Did you went to the doctor?" But we don't consider these utterances as errors—things that are wrong with children's speech. All of the above sentences could be the result of normal development of a first language within a child.

Mistakes are a natural and even necessary aspect of language learning. Mistakes are often the only way to get feedback from other people on your linguistic progress. When you goof in speaking the second language, you usually get some sort of response (a quizzical look, a question, a correction) that lets you know there was something in your language that wasn't quite right. Mistakes are not shameful. They are helpful, overt manifestations of a genuine attempt on your part to convey a message.

The joy of goofing

In the case of the verse at the beginning of this chapter, the mistakes in it were at worst irrelevant to the message, and at best they enhanced the message in unconventional ways. Our language goofs are sometimes the source of wonderful, tension-relieving humor.

I've been teaching English as a second language for many years now, and one of the greatest joys is laughing with—not at—students when they make mistakes. The delightful slips of the tongue and faux pas that students come up with provide both teacher and students with a lighter side of language learning.

I couldn't help smiling when one of my ESL students stood up and in a serious tone said, "Allow me to introduce myself and tell you about the headlights of my past." Another student came up with this rendition of a familiar proverb, "All work without a play makes Jack a doornail." Or even more striking, "The Washington Monument is the highest erection in the city." (I'm sure no one could dispute that statement!)

As your language attempts go awry, just remember that you may be on the verge of establishing yourself as a first-rate comedian. And as you laugh at yourself, perhaps others will laugh with you. The joy of such blundering should help you take language learning less seriously and relieve some of the tension involved.

Goofs and mistakes

Not all second-language errors are created equal. You may be tempted to think that a mistake is a mistake, and that's that. But there is an important distinction you can make that will help you to look at your errors more creatively and flexibly.

Some errors are simply *goofs* and others are honest to goodness *mistakes.*[47] Goofs are the little errors that everyone makes, even in their native language, that aren't consistently repeated. They are just slips of the tongue or pen or whatever. Here are some goofs that native speakers of English have made:

> "That needs some thinking about; let me go away and regurgitate for a couple of hours."
> "We didn't sleep very well last night; it was one of those castrated beds, and it kept rolling around."
> "In accordance with your instructions, I have given birth to twins in the enclosed envelope."

In all probability, the speakers or writers here could have corrected themselves if their goofs had been pointed out to them. And that just happens to be the major operational distinction between a goof and a mistake. Goofs, when they're pointed out to us, are visible and correctable. Mistakes, by definition, are not. Look at these sentences produced by students of ESL:

> "The teacher was so good the students were nailed to his lips."
> "He passed out with flying colors."
> "The temple elephants are paraded, and crackers burst throughout the night."

In each of these three delightful instances, the speakers were able to understand their errors immediately when they were pointed out, and everyone had a good laugh.

In contrast, here are a couple of sentences in which mistakes appear that were too complicated for the students to understand or correct:

> "In these lakes many kinds of famous fishes are living. These fishes are serving in the restaurants near by the lakes."
> "I like Abraham Lincoln, because he has known many people in Japan."

The importance of the distinction between goofs and mistakes is that you can listen for your goofs and profit from them. When you goof, normally you can hear it and then backtrack and try again. When you make a mistake, you may not be aware of it because mistakes occur even when you are making your best conscious attempt to speak the language correctly. They arise out of a system of second-language rules that is gradually forming in your head. It takes time for this system to develop within you, and you need to be patient with the process. When you do finally become aware that a rule in your head doesn't fit or is incorrect, you have to be willing to throw that rule out and possibly revamp your system of rules. Mistakes thus act as windows to your own conception of how the second language works. The windows allow you to see your own language performance and to take corrective action.

Where do mistakes come from?

In order to take corrective action, it is most helpful to know where your mistakes come from. There are four principal sources of mistakes: (1) your native language, (2) the second language itself, (3) the context of your learning situation, and (4) the strategies that you employ.

Your native language

Anytime you learn something new, you draw on a backlog of experiences and knowledge to assist you. If you are just learning to ski, for example, you will bring to that new experience a number of skills previously learned: walking, running, sledding down a hill, balancing on a railroad track, skateboarding, ice-skating, and so forth. As you try to keep your balance and do other maneuvers on skis, you transfer your previous experiences to the present one.

The situation isn't much different in learning a second language. It's just that the previously learned skill is your native language. Since you know your own language well, you are naturally inclined to map the new language skills directly onto the old. People do this on a variety of levels.

The sound system.   The sounds of the native language are assumed to work for the second language. If you are learning French, you tend to produce an American *r* rather than a French one; when saying *un peu* (a little), you lean toward pronouncing it "oon poo" or some such fractured form.

Grammatical system. Your native English grammar maps itself onto the new language. If you are studying German, you may be inclined to say "*Ich kann sprechen Deutsch*" rather than the correct "*Ich kann Deutsch sprechen*" (I can speak German). Your English word order becomes your guide.

Vocabulary. Words that you know in English get transferred in order to fill the gaps. A beginner in Spanish once tried to ask for the time by saying "*A que tiempo es?*" (What time is it?), not at that moment realizing that the correct word in Spanish is *hora* (hour), not *tiempo* (time).

You also tend to follow native-language norms of social appropriateness (politeness, for example) which may be significantly different from those of the second language. In Japanese, a simple *arigato* (thank you) without a characteristic bow of the head and a *gozaimasu* (politeness marker) may not display nearly enough gratitude for certain favors. In English, a simple "thank you" could be quite appropriate in a similar situation.

These *interlingual* errors of interference (the native language interfering with the second language) are usually the first mistakes to appear in your second-language learning journey. You have a natural tendency to plug the holes of your new language with the old. It is very hard to break away from the comfortable patterns you are used to. And sometimes, it's the more subtle differences between two languages that give you no end of trouble. False cognates, for example, can be difficult to remember. Consider Spanish words like *embarazado* and *constipado*. They do *not* mean "embarrassed" and "constipated"; rather, they mean "pregnant" and "to have a cold." Confusion surrounding such words has caused many a Spanish learner to blush.

Eventually, though, you'll make that breakthrough and feel suddenly liberated. You'll start thinking in the second language, and words and phrases will come off your tongue spontaneously.

Don't expect that breakthrough to come early. It takes a long time to feel that you have left your native language behind. But as you progress, the interference of the grammar, words, and social conventions of your native language will gradually diminish. Just don't forget that the interference of the sound system of English, in the form of a foreign accent, will probably never completely disappear.

The second language

Our errors frequently arise from the second language itself. These *intralingual* mistakes are the product of the complexity of the second language. Think of foreigners trying to learn English. You might hear them say things like, "I don't know what time is it," "My friend goed to the U.S.A. last year," or "Does John can sing?" Most likely these mistakes have occurred because the learner has become confused over a rule in English that has nothing to do with his or her native language. The rules for using verbs like *can, may, should,* and *would* are inherently difficult in English. The same is true of indirect statements and irregular past tenses.

The good news is that if you can identify your mistakes as stemming from the second language, it may indicate that you are on the road to thinking in the new language and making assumptions about how that language works. Such mistakes are typical of intermediate to advanced stages of second-language learning.

Context of learning

A third broad source of errors is the learning context, including all its personal and interpersonal variables. In the classroom, the most common context of learning a foreign language, consider the following possible sources of error:

- The teacher's own limitations in the foreign language may lead you to make some mistakes.
- The method of presentation or sequence of presentation may cause confusion. You may, for example, learn the terms *point at* and *point out* together and for many weeks or months have difficulty remembering which is which.
- The textbook you use might give misleading or confusing explanations that lead to a mistake.

- Other students in the class may reinforce your own mistakes and these mistakes may go unnoticed.
- You might learn a formal or bookish way of saying things that give you away as a classroom language learner.

Learning strategies

A fourth source of mistakes is the whole host of strategies that you as a learner employ in the process of trying to make the language your own. A typical ploy of the new language learner is to memorize common expressions for daily living ("How much does this cost?" "Where is the toilet?" etc.). Memorizing such phrases can produce embarrassing errors. In the early stages of learning the Kikongo language in Africa, I tried to say in Kikongo, "I don't know Kikongo," (*Kizeyi Kikongo ko*) to those who attempted to converse with me beyond my limits. I was later embarrassed to discover that my first few attempts to produce this little memorized chunk of language came out as, "I don't *like* Kikongo." (*Kizolele Kikongo ko.*) This was obviously not well received by my listeners.

One of my American colleagues tells the story of a time in Japan when she was eating with friends at a restaurant. She wanted to compliment the waiter on the food and asked one of her companions for the word meaning "great." Her friend gave her the word *oishi*, which actually means "delicious" and applies to food. Later in the evening at a night club, when an attractive young man finished an especially appealing performance of a romantic song, she yelled out to him above the din of the crowd "oishi!" That brought the house down.

There are other strategies that can end up working against you: paraphrasing to get around a difficult construction, translating or borrowing, using mime or nonverbal signals, appealing for assistance from someone else, and using a bilingual dictionary.

The bilingual dictionary is sometimes an especially unreliable source of knowledge. Once, at our university's foreign student office, a married couple wanted to find out from the receptionist if the two of them could live together in a dormitory room. Searching in their

Figure 13

bilingual dictionary for some way to say "live together," they finally came up with the question, "Can we copulate in dormitory room?" Needless to say, the red-faced receptionist didn't quite know how to answer them.

Remember, of course, the fact that because certain strategies may cause you to goof or make a mistake is no reason to avoid using them. A few mistakes are risks well worth taking.

Fossilization

In the best of all possible worlds, you always proceed steadily along the pathway of learning toward the ultimate goal of being able to communicate in the language. Even though your progress chart has little ups and downs as you move along, you want to think of yourself as showing a general upward growth trend.

Unfortunately, it doesn't always happen that way. One common occurrence among language learners is for language to "plateau out," frequently referred to as *fossilization*. Fossilization in language learning, like its geological namesake, is a process by which an incorrect form solidifies or is ingrained by habit in a learner's repertoire. How many people do you think actually progress steadily through the beginning, intermediate, and advanced stages of language learning and just keep on going without a hitch or pause until they've reached virtual native-speaker competence? Very few. Most learners will progress to a point where at least part of what they have learned fossilizes. Why? Usually because the learner is reasonably satisfied with his or her proficiency and/or the process of learning has become unrewarding.

Fossilized language learning is found frequently among immigrants in a country where the language spoken is different from their own. For a few months—or years—the immigrants, in a state of high motivation, plunge into the new language and culture. Reasonably good progress is made as they hear and use the language daily and attend night school classes. But then they grow comfortable with the degree of skill they have developed, which may be sufficient for the job they have and for meeting their everyday needs. Their motivation for further learning diminishes.

Fossilization can even occur while you are taking classes. Despite pressure from teachers and fellow students, it's easy to grow weary of the grind and allow certain language competencies to fossilize. So, no matter what your context of learning is, mistakes can creep into your language system and fossilize. You don't attempt to correct your mistakes because you have grown comfortable with them. They get you what you want. You have little or no motivation for further improvement. You are happy on your plateau.

Can fossilization be prevented? Once it appears to have set in, can you "unfossilize?" In both cases, the answer is yes. Since fossilization is largely caused by the way you perceive your own needs, that is, by your own level of motivation, you can engage in various tricks to keep yourself pressing on toward higher and higher goals.

One key to prevention is to process the feedback you receive as you interact with others. Look for verbal and nonverbal signals from others as you speak. Most people are tolerant of someone who is trying to communicate in their language. They will ignore errors as they try to understand even fractured communication.

At the same time, people do give corrective feedback, which in its simplest form[48] can be categorized as

- positive feedback: "I understand" (message is clear),
- neutral feedback: "I'm not sure I understand" (undecided), or
- negative feedback: "I don't understand" (message is not clear).

Positive feedback is usually manifested by various "uh huh" responses, nods of the head, and other facial expressions. Neutral feedback is ambiguous; you're not sure whether your message came across or not. Negative feedback isn't really negative, it's simply an indication that you haven't been understood. Negative feedback is actually the key to progress. As listeners question you, ask you to repeat, give you quizzical looks, and otherwise let you know that you are not coming through clearly, you will have the strongest stimulus to improve your skills.

Negative feedback provides information or data for your mental computer. It tells you that a word is wrong, a sentence unclear, the pronunciation garbled, or whatever. Processing this information enables you to identify where you need improvement. And it's important to watch carefully for negative feedback because people will all too frequently give you positive feedback in an effort not to embarrass you, even when they don't understand what you have said.

This kind of politeness can lead you seriously astray. You may have just enough competence to get most of your thoughts across so that people respond with positive signals. It is easy at that point to feel smug and think you have arrived. But you haven't, and if you want to continue your progress, you must look for the subtle signals that indicate that you are not communicating as well as you think you are.

Classroom error correction

The next question is what to do with the feedback you get, especially in that most common of language learning contexts, the classroom.

The previous discussion about fossilization and feedback referred basically to real-world, natural, untutored situations. In such contexts you won't get much direct correction, so you have to figure out how to correct yourself. You have to train yourself to notice certain mistakes, to zoom in on where you are going wrong. You may have to create your own disciplined program of selective attention to certain aspects of language. You may even have to explicitly request correction from people you converse with.

In the classroom things are quite different. Here the language environment is artificial, and a teacher is present to provide extensive feedback. At the same time you may encounter a wide variety of teaching styles and methods of conducting the class. Teachers' methods of error correction can range from correcting all your errors to correcting none of your errors. In between those extremes are various possibilities of pointing out errors in some way but not necessarily correcting them directly. Still other classroom approaches involve encouraging students to correct each other.

You probably have a preference for how you might like the teacher to handle error correction. However, your preference may not always be honored. Then what? With some luck, your teacher won't correct every little error you make. That will encourage you to keep talking, and you won't feel stifled and inhibited. But if your errors are never corrected, you won't get the feedback you need. In which case, you should actively solicit some sort of error feedback.

When you do get corrective feedback, take special note of what it was you said or wrote, and use those aspects of language as an agenda for subsequent study. In so doing, you will take some small steps of your own toward eliminating errors. You may need to work on errors one by one, category by category. Maybe one week you work on articles, the next, verb tenses, and so on. As you work on your mistakes, remember that you must not get too hung up on the fact that you are making them. Mistakes are windows to your language competence. You have the power to make your mistakes work *for* you rather than against you.

What can your mistakes do for you?

In this chapter we have seen that mistakes are a natural part of second-language learning and can be important indicators of your progress. Some tips to remember:

1. Your mistakes can be a source of pleasure and amusement; cultivate the ability to laugh at yourself and with others, as you enjoy the lighter side of learning.
2. Try to distinguish between errors that are just goofs or slip-ups that you can easily correct and mistakes that seem to be a part of a pattern. Work on the mistakes in some systematic way.
3. Many of your mistakes will come from your native language. Try to recognize when they do and see if you can shift into thinking directly in the second language.
4. Some mistakes will stem from the complexity of the second language itself. They are probably an indication of your growing competence.

5. Still other mistakes will be a product of your learning environment. Watch out for some of the pitfalls of class-room-induced errors: teachers' errors, confusing textbook explanations, and even errors made by other students in your class.

6. Use a variety of communication strategies: memorizing routines, paraphrasing, translating, using mime, asking others for help, and consulting a bilingual dictionary. Keep in mind, however, that these strategies themselves can lead to some errors.

7. Fossilization is a natural occurrence in second-language learning. You can plateau out at certain points unless you keep your motivation high and stay alert to reading as many feedback signals as possible.

8. Be prepared in a classroom context for a number of different teacher styles of error correction. Make the best of whatever style your teacher uses by staying attuned to the feedback you get so that your mistakes work for you and not against you.

9

Choosing Your Classroom Method

Twenty students have trekked through a snowstorm to be on time for their 8:00 A.M. French class.[49] Their eyes widen as the door is flung open and a hunched figure, dressed in black, shuffles into the classroom with his back to the class. With a moan the figure whirls around displaying a sweaty face contorted in agony and splotched with white.

"*Ah, mes frères,*" he cries, "*J'ai découvert la vérité!*"

The figure is Professor John Rassias of Dartmouth College, and he's portraying a character in one of Claudel's plays who has just journeyed to hell and back. Rassias continues his monologue, which soon becomes a dialogue with his students as the play comes alive, and as language becomes a vehicle for conveying real feelings within the students in the classroom.

According to Rassias, second-language learning should be like the fires of hell, burning away the inhibition that blocks communication and the prejudice that prevents sensitivity. His classes are well known for their drama. On one day he wears a blonde wig, playing the part of Denis

Diderot, a French philosopher. On another day he grabs a chair and flings it against the wall to demonstrate a hero's anger in a short story. On yet another, students are told to wear grocery sacks over their heads to simulate what it's like not to be able to see.

Rassias draws a parallel between teaching and acting. The teacher and actor must both give themselves totally to the audience. In language learning, this relationship is especially important because students, with their growing new identities, are also actors.

You may not have the good fortune to be taught a foreign language by John Rassias. But there are superior language teachers out there using a variety of successful methods. In this chapter, we will take a look at some of those methods and get a sense of what the options are, what's good about them, and what to be wary of. Perhaps, then, if you have the opportunity to choose a teacher or a method, you will have some criteria with which to judge the suitability of your future language learning experience.

Imagine, now, that you are visiting a world's fair. You discover that one of the pavilions in the fair is called "Languages of the World" and that one wing of this pavilion displays up-to-date information on methods of language teaching. Perfect, you surmise, for here you can readily get information that will help you choose a teacher or a method. As you browse through the pavilion, here is what you might see and hear.

"Wrong way" François Gouin

The first exhibit you encounter focuses on the history of language teaching. The designers have chosen to begin that history with the amusing but poignant story of how one of the first language teaching methods was born, the story of François Gouin.[50]

François Gouin (we'll call him François) was a teacher of Latin who lived in France in the nineteenth century. A year or two before 1880, François decided he needed to learn German. So he took a year away from his teaching job in France and went to Hamburg. Borrowing from his methods of teaching Latin, François decided that the best way to learn German would be to memorize a German grammar book and the 248 irregular German verbs. He isolated himself in his room for ten days, and successfully memorized the book and the verbs. Emerging from his ten-day isolation, he wished to test his new linguistic knowledge. He hurried to the university and went from one class to the next. Gouin recounts his experience:

> But alas! In vain did I strain my ears; in vain my eye strove to interpret the slightest movements of the lips of the professor; in vain I passed from the first classroom to a second; not a word, not a single word would penetrate to my understanding. Nay more than this, I did not even distinguish a single one of the grammatical forms so newly studied; I did not recognize even a single one of the irregular verbs just freshly learnt, though they certainly must have fallen in crowds from the lips of the speaker.

Well, François wasn't about to give up. So back to his room he went. This time, remembering how he learned Greek by tackling the Greek roots, he decided to memorize eight hundred German roots—and of course to rememorize the grammar book and irregular verbs. He was convinced that this go-around would surely offer him "the foundations of the language, as well as the laws and secret of its forms, regular and irregular." After eight days he hurried again to the university. "But alas!" He understood not one word.

The stubbornness of our dear Latin teacher now becomes painfully evident. He was relatively undaunted by his first two failures to learn German. Next he tried what should have been a successful strategy: he tried talking with the customers in the shop below his room. But they laughed at him, and embarrassed, sensitive François decided to return to the solitude of his room. This time he tried translating Goethe and Schiller—but alas! Next, he spent three weeks memorizing a book of dialogues—but alas! Then he spent a full month memorizing the thirty thousand words of a dictionary—but alas! And this time he went on to add: "...I understood not a word—not a single word!...and I permit no one to doubt the sincerity of this statement. Not a word!" He was still not ready to give up. He tried reading again. He memorized the dictionary again and later a third time. All to no avail.

Finally, his year-long stay came to an end, and François left Germany without ever having learned to speak or understand German. He had, in no uncertain terms, completely and utterly failed in his effort.

Fortunately, there was a relatively happy ending to the story. Upon his return home François found that his little three-year-old nephew had gone through that wonderful, miraculous stage of first-language acquisition in which children, in the course of sometimes less than a year, move from two-year-old "telegraphese" to nonstop chatterboxes of language. François perceived that his nephew possessed a secret of some sort and set out to study child language acquisition. His studies revealed many insights about child language acquisition, from which François concluded that he and all other language teachers were teaching the wrong way. He invented a method called the *Series Method,* a direct, conversational approach with no grammatical analysis, no vocabulary memorization, and no translation.

François Gouin's Series Method never became widely used, partly because Gouin was not the entrepreneur that his colleague Charles Berlitz was. Gouin's ideas and methods were the early inspiration for Berlitz, whose famous *Direct Method* enjoyed popularity in the early 1900s and whose schools are still thriving. We can nevertheless happily end the story of "wrong-way François" by noting that the excruciating pain of his year-long efforts to learn German eventually led to positive ends. Thus are some methods born.

The Grammar-Translation Method

As you move along through the historical exhibit, you see that despite the insights of people like Gouin—and, a few years later, Berlitz—traditional methods, with their emphasis on memorization, grammar, and translation, nevertheless prevailed. Conversational methods, with their tutorial or small-class approach, were too costly. And so language teaching in both Europe and the United States remained dominated by what is called the *Grammar-Translation Method.*

If you have already taken a foreign language in high school or college, you may have had the misfortune of suffering through a class taught by the grammar-translation method. Grammar-translation classes consist mainly of learning rules of grammar, reading and translating passages word for word, doing grammatical exercises, and memorizing vocabulary lists. Classes are conducted in your native tongue. You rarely hear any sustained conversation in the foreign language itself. Accuracy is emphasized, especially in written exercises. A good deal of class time is spent discussing grammatical points—especially those intricate and obscure exceptions to the rules that fascinate teachers and thoroughly bamboozle students.

The Audiolingual Method

As you walk along the historical displays, you discover that a second strand of language learning tradition was actually quite revolutionary when it began. After World War II, Americans experienced a sudden awareness that they were on a shrinking globe and were much too ignorant of other languages. Responding to the need to train military personnel to converse in foreign languages, the Department of Defense developed a methodology which was based on the methods of Gouin and Berlitz and which focused on the spoken language. Originally referred to as the *Army Method*, it consisted of a very intensive six- to eight-hour-a-day program utilizing a *mimicry and memorization*, or *oral-aural* approach.

Universities and foreign language organizations were soon advocating and adopting the method. While schools were not always able to provide the intensive instruction the army did, they nevertheless began to introduce oral-aural techniques into their language classrooms. By the midcentury mark, the new oral-aural approach, ultimately known as the *Audiolingual Method* (ALM), was widely acclaimed by professional language educators. The ALM advocated great quantities of oral activity in the classroom in the form of memorized dialogues and drills. Overlearning, habit formation, and repetition were key features. Educators and behavioral psychologists argued that we learn by doing and not by analyzing and that language is a habit that needs to be formed by practice, practice, and more practice.

Figure 14

This theory of language learning soon gave rise to widespread construction and use of a new technology: audio language laboratories. In the language lab, students sat in booths and listened to a multiplicity of tapes of native speakers reading textbook vocabulary, sentences, and conversations. Most labs featured recording equipment so that students could record their attempts to mimic the speaker on the tape. Some hailed the language lab as the ultimate language teaching tool.

The ALM was popular for some time. It was refreshing for learners to get away from the analysis and heady mental gymnastics of grammar-translation. People could simulate conversations by repeating their memorized routines. In the privacy of a language lab booth, students could listen ad nauseam to native speakers and try to loosen their tongues. Americans did indeed become sensitized to the spoken languages of the world.

But by the early 1970s, the glitter of the ALM had worn off. People weren't really speaking languages; they were mouthing them. They weren't really developing conversational fluency; they were memorizing empty patterns. And language labs, which kept breaking down with annoying predictability, only reinforced rote learning. Many schools returned to the safety of grammar-translation while others attempted to blend the two methods.

The language teaching profession was ripe for another revolution. While some pushed for a noisy, confrontational rebellion, others more appropriately advocated a quieter, more balanced exploration of alternative methodologies.

As you continue to peruse the language teaching exhibits in your tour of the fair, you encounter displays of current trends and options, which you can now place against the backdrop of a century of language teaching.

Home study programs

Convenience, self-paced schedules, rapid learning, low cost— these are some of the catchwords you find in a booth full of home study programs. You are tempted to believe you need to go no further. For as little as $15 or as much as $295, you are promised miracles as you go from display to display. It is here that you find the advertisement mentioned in chapter 1 that says, "What would you give to learn a foreign language? Try $125." And for that price, they even throw in a cassette tape player and a handsome attaché case.

Before you invest even a small sum in a program like this, consider some of the limitations. First, it is not possible to become fluent or anything close to it in a matter of a few weeks of listening to cassette tapes, much less a few days or hours as some seem to claim. If the program is well designed and provides a progression of listening activities in which you eventually hear natural language in conversational settings, then you can get a sense of what that language sounds like. If you are reasonably good at mimicking, a self-study program may help you to produce a few useful survival phrases. But you won't develop any significant degree of proficiency by means of these programs alone.

Second, home study programs fail to provide the absolutely essential ingredient for language learning: another person with whom you can interact in the language. You should always consider a home study program as something that supplements other experiences. It can act as an initial stimulus or an additional set of materials along with a regular language class. Many people have found the phrase-book-plus-tape a useful item to work with before taking a trip somewhere or before enrolling in a language class. But nothing substitutes for real people with whom you can carry on purposeful conversations.

One of the booths you stroll by next is sponsored by the National Association for Self-Instructional Language Programs (NASILP). Here you find brochures on correspondence courses. Should you consider enrolling in a correspondence course in a foreign language? Some of the same limitations apply: you won't achieve fluency in a language without people to interact with. A correspondence course, however, can give you some knowledge about the grammar of a language and some ability to read it. If you are studying a second language just to pass some sort of written test, a good correspondence course might help you to improve your test performance.

As you leave this exhibit, you pick up a list of sources you can turn to for more information.

Self-study courses:

> Foreign Service Institute
> Catalog of Language Courses
> Order Section
> National Audio-Visual Center
> General Services Administration
> Washington, DC 20409

> Audio-Forum
> Suite 33
> On the Green
> Guilford, CT 06437

> Educational Services Corporation
> 1725 K Street, NW, Suite 408
> Washington, DC 20006

Correspondence courses:

> National Association of
> Self-Instructional Language Programs
> Box 38, Humanities Building
> Temple University
> Philadelphia, PA 19122

Berlitz language schools

The next exhibit features the worldwide chain of Berlitz language schools. Charles Berlitz was one of the first people to commercialize language teaching. At the turn of the century his Direct Method was a radical departure from the prevailing instructional methods. Instead of grammar work, translation, vocabulary memorization, dull reading, and even duller writing exercises, a Berlitz language course offered a refreshingly different approach:

- The teacher conducted the class exclusively in the foreign language.
- Everyday vocabulary and sentences were taught.
- Speaking and listening were emphasized through a sequence of sentence patterns and question-and-answer exchanges between student and teacher.
- Grammar was not taught specifically, only inductively.
- There was no translation. The teacher introduced new words and sentences through demonstration.
- Classes were kept small and intensive (three to four hours a day).

In the early 1900s a Berlitz school was an attractive alternative to traditional classes where foreign languages were treated like any other school subject. Unfortunately, the Berlitz alternative was a costly one since small classes and unsubsidized private language schools were expensive to operate.

Today, Berlitz language schools are found all over the world, and they still use the same teaching method that was used in 1900. Their emphasis on conversation and on minimizing explicit grammar and memorization is a positive facet. They are still on the expensive side, largely because of the cost of conducting very small classes. But they are no longer the only bastion of innovation. Language courses with small classes and a conversational emphasis can be found elsewhere, even in high school and university courses. What was revolutionary in 1900 is no longer so today.

For information on Berlitz language courses, you can consult telephone directories in most large cities in the U.S. There are about seventy schools across the country. If you don't find anything listed, you can get information from

Berlitz Language Schools
Research Park
293 Wall Street
Princeton, NJ 08540

The next cluster of booths represents language teaching methods that have more recently appeared on the scene. The last two decades of research on second-language acquisition have spawned some innovative instructional techniques which broaden the range of viable choices open to you. Some of the newer methods have been created by independent commercial language schools. As you look over the displays, here is what you find.

Suggestopedia

You have already been introduced to *Suggestopedia* in chapter 4. Suggestopedia promises you an enjoyable experience, one where you learn in a relaxed state of mind, almost effortlessly. You will presumably learn great quantities of material in a short time. There will be daily concert sessions—in which dialogues are read aloud against the backdrop of baroque music. There will be speaking activities in each class session. You will engage in role plays and skits and interaction activities.

Chapter 4 presented a number of the limitations of the suggestopedic approach. You do yourself a favor not to be drawn into any method too quickly. Suggestopedia may appear to be quite irresistible if you only look at the trimmings. After you get used to listening to foreign language conversations with a Mozart violin concerto playing in the background, the class sessions may not seem so innovative. Yes, drama is an important component of the method, but you also do a little bit of translating and grammar learning and engage in singing and other kinds of relatively standard communication activities. In the final analysis, the expertise and dynamism of your teacher is more likely to determine the success of the class than its suggestopedic content or structure.

Community Language Learning

The next booth intrigues you. A demonstration lesson on a video monitor shows a small group of about eight students sitting in a circle—Americans learning Arabic. The teacher is standing outside the circle. A student says, in English, "It's sunny today." The teacher comes around and quietly translates the sentence into Arabic, which the student repeats in Arabic. A second student responds in English, "Yes, but not very warm," and the teacher translates for her, with the student repeating again in Arabic. This goes on for some time as students initiate conversation in English but always get an immediate translation in Arabic, which they repeat and direct to another student.

As you fast-forward through the demonstration tape you find that several weeks into this course students are beginning to carry on some of their own conversation in Arabic without requiring translation by the teacher. Much later, the teacher may become more of a prompter and guide than a translator. Conversation sessions are always followed by comments from the teacher on points of grammar illustrated by the sentences that the class initiated.

In a *Community Language Learning* (CLL) class, you are supported by a small community of learners. You can rely on your native language whenever you want, but when you are ready, you can use the second language. You can determine what you want to say; no one will dictate the sentences you have to use. You and your classmates form a closely knit group of kindred souls who aid each other in the process of learning, while the teacher assumes the role of a counselor.

This method, too, looks enticing. But there are some drawbacks, especially if you are a beginning language learner. Your group can end up floundering for weeks without making progress as you grope for linguistic structures. It is sometimes more efficient to allow a teacher or textbook to direct you through a manageable sequence of basic learning. And relying exclusively on translation to derive meanings in the early stages of your language course can be misleading and confusing. Once you have a basic grasp of the language, then you might profit more from a modified CLL approach, in which the teacher guides your conversation and doesn't rely so heavily on translation.

The Silent Way

A group of observers is forming at the next booth. You are invited to join a "guinea pig" class of six people who will "learn" French. You've never taken French, so you accept the challenge and sit down at a table with a teacher who dumps out a bag full of small colored rods of various lengths (Cuisenaire rods, often used to teach math concepts to children). The teacher, somewhat expressionless, picks up a red rod and says *"rouge."* The students are silent. With blue, yellow, and green rods, the teacher says *"bleu," "jaune," "vert."* Students remain silent. Without saying anything, the teacher hands the red rod to you. Silence. The teacher waits. After an uncomfortably long period of quiet, you figure you'd better do something with the red rod so you pass it to another student. The others laugh. The teacher merely smiles. Hesitantly, the person with the rod ventures to say "roodge." The teacher frowns a bit. Another student nonverbally asks for the rod, takes it, and says "rouge." The teacher smiles approvingly. Other students now try saying "rouge."

The procedure continues inductively with other colored rods. Then the teacher holds up two rods and says *"deux."* And then with three, *"trois,"* and so forth, through five. The group begins to get into the game, even to the point of someone venturing to say *"deux rouge,"* and *"trois bleu."* Before long, the teacher is modeling little sentences like *"J'ai trois rouges baguettes"* (I have three red rods), and students are expanding to other colors and numbers.

You have just participated in a demonstration of the *Silent Way.* Here the teacher is relatively silent, giving the students the responsibility of memorizing, correcting, and maintaining conversation. The teacher also remains somewhat impassive in order to encourage students to generate their own motivation. As you look at the literature in the booth, you see that subsequent stages of the Silent Way involve the use of elaborate grammar charts and extensive conversations using not just the

Cuisenaire rods but other props as well. However, as you examine those later lessons, you note that they seem to lose their distinctiveness as a separate and unique method.

The Silent Way catches your attention at the outset. You become engrossed in the process of carefully attending to the few utterances the teacher makes. You also enjoy the mutual supportiveness of your peers, as together you try to figure out meanings. In spite of minimal input from the teacher, you feel the potential for making fairly rapid progress is good. But you may be disappointed as the lessons wear on. You can easily get bogged down in grammar, vocabulary, repetition, and rote practice—not unlike what you would find in the Audiolingual Method. So, if you are looking for a quick entry into the language, the Silent Way can be helpful and fun for a couple of weeks. But if your aim is eventual fluency, it becomes quite traditional after a short time.

For more information on the above three commercial language programs, write to

Suggestopedia:

    Society for Accelerative Learning & Teaching (SALT)
    Department of Psychology, W-112 Lago Marcino
    Iowa State University
    Ames, IA 50011-3180

Community Language Learning:

    Counseling-Learning Institutes
    P.O. Box 285
    East Dubuque, IL 61025

The Silent Way:

    Educational Solutions
    95 University Place
    New York, NY 10003

Total immersion language programs

The next exhibit offers yet another approach to language learning. We have already seen in earlier chapters that one of the best ways to learn a second language is to engage in some sort of sink-or-swim method, where you jump into the deep end of the pool and "swim" like crazy. In keeping with this spirit, some programs offer an intensive total immersion experience. One display describes a typical immersion program offered at Middlebury College in Vermont, where eight-week summer courses are conducted in Arabic, Chinese, French, German, Italian, Japanese, Russian, and Spanish. In those programs you live and breathe the foreign language twenty-four hours a day. You live in a house or dorm where only the target language is spoken and where English is definitely taboo. Similar courses are offered at a few other universities and at such specialized institutions as the Monterey Institute of International Studies.

If you have six or eight weeks to devote exclusively to the language you want to learn, the total immersion program is an excellent way to go. By forcing you to survive in the language, immersion programs simulate living in the country where it is spoken. And with few distractions around you, you can make rapid progress. If your teacher and tutors are well trained in methodology and if the program is administered to provide a maximum of interaction, you can hardly go wrong. Try to find out ahead of time the level of expertise of your teachers and the extent to which you will really be totally immersed and not just halfway dunked into the language. Ask former students about the program's effectiveness. If the signals are all positive, you stand to gain a great deal. For more information write to

The Sunderland Language Schools
Middlebury College
Middlebury, VT 05753

Monterey Institute of International Studies
Department of Language Studies
425 Van Buren Street
Monterey, CA 93940

Computerized language lessons

As you round the corner, you encounter a group of booths with a multiplicity of computer terminals and monitors. Fair-goers are sitting at the terminals, fiddling with the keys and running various language programs. Now, you think, I'm approaching ultimate truth! Computers have solved so many of the world's communication problems, why shouldn't they be the final answer to foreign language learning?

Good question. Unfortunately, the answer isn't as unequivocal as you might wish. In the fifties and early sixties, the language teaching profession saluted the technological wonders of the language laboratory as the ultimate in bringing electronics and language learning together. But, as we have already noted, we soon discovered that a row of booths with tape recorders didn't necessarily create a successful language program.

Today, some are ready to jump onto the computer bandwagon with similar gusto. The advantage of self-pacing programs, especially if coordinated with an audio soundtrack, is not to be overlooked. The fascination of working with a computer program is a great motivator. But it would be premature to conclude that the computer is at this time ready to provide the advances in language teaching technology that we may look forward to in the future. The software is still in an early developmental stage. Much of it is mechanical and repetitious, as the computer user simply works through computerized versions of paper-and-pencil exercises.

At the present time, one of the best uses of computers in a language course is as a focal point for a small group of learners. By focusing on an adventure game or on an educational program, students communicate with each other—in the foreign language—in order to solve a particular problem. In so doing, they are practicing meaningful use of the language.

A new development in computerization that holds future promise for language learners is *interactive video*. Here, the learner is presented with videotaped scenarios in the second language. A computer program interacts with the video input to allow the learner to respond on the computer keyboard to preprogrammed questions related to the videotape scenario.

In one such program that you see displayed in this exhibit, Japanese businessmen are taught basic English in a scenario called "Flight 509." The first scene includes boarding the flight, in-flight conversations, arrival in San Francisco, customs, hotel check-in; the next scene depicts the following morning's business meeting. Throughout, learners respond to a myriad of options that allow them to create their own story. For example, when the customs officer says, "Do you have anything to declare?" the learner can type yes or no on the computer. Each response will then trigger different follow-up scenes.

So far, the major disadvantage of interactive video is that the learner cannot actually speak into the computer; all the learner input has to be typed. Some day in the not-too-distant future, computer programs will have the capacity to "understand" spoken language. Even now, computers can process human language that has been prerecorded, but the computer recognizes the sounds produced only by a particular person. When computers are able to process new voices struggling with a brand-new language, then we will indeed have arrived!

For up-to-date information on the applications of computers for language learning, write to

Computer Assisted Language Instruction Consortium
(CALICO)
3078 JKHB
Brigham Young University
Provo, UT 84602
Telephone: 801-378-7079

Finding the eclectic ideal

As you leave the onlookers crowded around the interactive video, you become aware of the buzz of conversation around you. Some of the conversations are in languages other than English, and you are reminded of the universally human, dynamic nature of language. Language is used for interaction among real, unpredictable human beings. The marvels of computer and other technologies are able to supplement communicative language lessons but can never replace meaningful, live, human interaction.

But by now your head is spinning with everything you have seen, and you have probably come to the conclusion that no single method is completely suitable for your particular needs and means. What then can you get from this tour that will guide you in choosing a foreign language class and/or teacher?

The current state of the art in language teaching methodology can best be described as cautiously eclectic. After a century of modern approaches to language teaching, we have learned that there is no single method that will work for all people in all situations. Most language courses will therefore contain a mixture of different approaches. The course in which you are most likely to succeed will have an eclectic blend of methods and techniques designed to maximize your chances of learning. Can you find such a course? What should you look for?

How to choose your language course

The last exhibit in this language teaching wing may just have the answer: twelve practical criteria for choosing a language course.

1. The teacher is a warm, lively communicator who obviously enjoys people and shows a zest for the job.
2. The teacher has a fluent command of the foreign language and can therefore use the language in a wide variety of contexts.
3. The teacher has professional training in language teaching methodology (just because someone knows the foreign language doesn't mean he or she is automatically a good teacher). The teacher must be familiar with a variety of methods and techniques and willing to adapt and blend

these methods to suit the particular class and the goals of the course.

4. The course focuses on meaningful, real-life communication among people instead of primarily emphasizing grammar, individual sounds, and explanations about how the language works.

5. Memorization and other forms of rote learning are either absent or used sparingly. Instead, through small group work and other spontaneous modes of communication, you are encouraged to speak the language, even if your attempts aren't perfect. You are thereby motivated to achieve some fluency in the language.

6. You are urged to be as accurate as possible in developing clear, effective communication. While native-speaker perfection is not necessarily the goal, you are encouraged to strive for your highest potential.

7. Lively, current, contextualized materials are able to keep you motivated and fascinated. As you immerse yourself in the content of the course (topics of conversation, textbooks, films, videos, other audiovisuals), the language itself develops subconsciously and efficiently.

8. Translation into or from English is kept to a bare minimum. You are encouraged from the first day to use the foreign language as exclusively as possible. English is used sparingly for certain explanations, cultural notes, and for filling other gaps where the foreign language would be over your head.

9. The class is clearly student-centered. The teacher is an important force in guiding, encouraging, correcting, and giving other forms of feedback, but from the outset the focus is primarily on you, the student.

10. There is plenty of room for a variety of levels of ability among the students in the class. The teacher provides supplementary work in the form of audiotapes, computer programs, workbook exercises, and so on, for those who are either well above or well below the norm for the course.

11. The course content is balanced among speaking, listening, reading, and writing.
12. Classes are relatively small. If your class is larger than fifteen, your turn comes up too infrequently and the teacher's ability to give you feedback is severely hampered.

Finding a course that meets all twelve criteria may be difficult; however, taken separately, they are not impossible ideals. Language courses that meet these criteria may be thought of as belonging to a general approach in language teaching known as *Communicative Language Teaching*, which is in many ways an ideal blend of methods, both current and past. The twelve criteria are, in a sense, a summary of the best of what we now know about second-language learning. They are presented to you as a checklist to guide your choice of an effective foreign language course. Good luck!

10

CREATING
YOUR OWN PATHWAY

The spirit of self-help is the root of all genuine growth in the individual; and, exhibited in the lives of many, it constitutes the true source of national vigor and strength. Help from without is often enfeebling in its effects, but help from within invariably invigorates.

—SAMUEL SMILES, *Self-Help,* 1859

This book has prodded you, I hope, to do something to control your own destiny in the awesome task of learning another language. You may be in a classroom—where a teacher commands, directs, guides, or facilitates. Or you may be trying to learn a language on your own. In either case, you can take specific measures to create your own pathway to success.

Your first step is to understand yourself—to discover what inner capacities you have that will help you to go about the process. As you have been reading this book, you have no doubt been doing

some intuitive self-assessment. As you read about ambiguity tolerance, for example, you may have thought, "All these language rules
sure throw me for a loop sometimes, so I should probably learn to
take things a step at a time." Or you might have concluded, "I'm a
pretty systematic, analytical thinker—I'd better not get too hung up
on grammatical analysis as I learn the language."

These assessments are somewhat informal. In this chapter you
will have a chance to do some self-tests that are more systematic.
The tests may reveal some surprises, but they should also confirm at
least some of your hunches about your styles of learning and thinking.
Your scores may give you a little better idea of what kind of language
learner you are—what your *"language quotient "*is. You can then
draw implications for your future language learning efforts.

Without reading further, go to the Appendix and take the five
paper-and-pencil tests included there. You will find instructions for
marking your responses and for scoring them. Once you have done
that, then resume reading here. If you continue reading the rest of
this chapter without taking the tests, you won't get a candid, unbiased
set of measures.

Go to tests in the Appendix on page 159

Testing your styles and strategies

What you have just taken is a battery of tests designed to give
you an indication of some of your personal and mental styles of
interacting with other people and of dealing with problems. Obviously these tests don't cover everything we have talked about in this
book, but they do focus on several topics that have an important
bearing on the degree of success you will have in learning a foreign
language.

There are some important limitations to tests of this kind. First,
keep in mind that all tests of cognitive styles are at best tentative and

that they indicate tendencies rather than fixed characteristics. Scores can be affected by a number of variables. The mood you were in when you took the tests could have colored some responses. The extent to which you may have tried to flatter yourself in some way could also have been a factor. For example, if you subconsciously felt that you should be more extroverted in your language learning, you may have slanted your answers a little on the first test. Virtually every "self-report" test (in which you have to make an assessment of yourself) has a liberal margin for error.

Second, these tests, as opposed to widely used, standardized self-report tests, are still experimental in nature. They have been validated on several groups of foreign language learners but not on thousands of learners across the country. Therefore, some caution is needed in interpreting your scores. Take them with a grain of salt. If the scores seem to be telling you something about yourself that you already suspected, so much the better. If not, you might seek out some other, similar tests on your own and see how well they match. For such consultation, some sources are given below.

Third, there is no such thing as a good style or a bad style. Extroversion, as you may remember from chapter 5, can be a positive factor, but an introvert has strengths that could be equally favorable. Right-brain dominance can work for you and against you. The point of these tests is not to find out, before the fact, if you are a good language learner. Everyone is potentially a good if not an excellent language learner. There are no inborn or immutable traits that spell doom to a would-be learner. If you want to learn a language, if you are willing to work at it with gusto, if you understand yourself well and then capitalize on your own unique mix of styles of thinking, feeling, and acting, then surely you will succeed. These self-tests are designed to help you continue the process of understanding yourself.

Test 1: Extroversion

This extroversion test was modeled after, and cross-validated with, two other widely used tests of extroversion.[51] While psychologists haven't by any means found a flawless way to measure extroversion, this test comes as close as any.

The higher your score on the test, the greater your extroversion. Remember, extroversion is the extent to which you need to interact with other people in order to feel sustained, whole, fulfilled, and happy. Introversion, indicated by the lower end of scores on this test, is the extent to which your emotional and mental needs are met on your own, without other people to interact with.

Here is how to interpret your score:

13 and above	quite extroverted
9 to 12	moderately extroverted
7 or 8	moderately introverted
6 and below	quite introverted

What are the implications for you as a language learner? If your score was 9 or above, indicating extroversion, try to capitalize on your need to be with others. Use that tendency to interact with people in the foreign language. Even if you fall flat on your face linguistically, you will probably derive enough emotional strength from others to keep trying. Group work in class should be your strength. A highly extroverted score, however, may mean that you don't do enough work on your own, such as studying aspects of the language that give you difficulty. You may be almost too willing to plunge in without considering carefully enough how the linguistic system works.

If you are on the introverted side of the scoring range, your strength is probably in thinking through aspects of the language and working on grammar and vocabulary on your own. Use your enjoyment of solitude to sort out the mysteries of language structures. At the same time, however, don't shy away from face-to-face communication. If group work and free conversation scare you a bit, try to work in small groups of two or three, where your inhibitions will be less likely to hamper your efforts. The systematic thinking that you do on your own will very likely pay off as you open up.

For further consultation, the following tests are recommended:

Myers-Briggs Type Indicator
Consulting Psychologists Press, Inc.
577 College Avenue
Palo Alto, CA 94306

Keirsey-Bates Temperament Sorter
(in *Please Understand Me*, by David Keirsey and Marilyn Bates)
Prometheus Nemesis Book Co.
Box 2082
Del Mar, CA 92014

Eysenck Personality Inventory
Educational and Industrial Testing Service
San Diego, CA 92107

Test 2: Ambiguity tolerance

As you may remember from chapter 5, ambiguity tolerance is also one of those factors that can work for or against you. It's not hard to see the value of being able to tolerate ambiguity when you find yourself surrounded by words, phrases, and expressions that you don't understand and can only hope to learn through a slow process of trial and error. At the same time, if you are so tolerant of ambiguity that nothing ever gets fixed in your mind, you will never master the system.

The higher your score on both parts of Test 2 (part A, items 1-18 and part B, items 19-25), the greater your ambiguity tolerance. A lower score indicates intolerance. Test 2A is a test of general or global ambiguity tolerance. Test 2B measures your ambiguity tolerance specifically in foreign language learning.

Here is how scores break down:

Test 2A	Test 2B	
60 and above	25 and above	quite tolerant of ambiguity
50 to 59	21 to 24	moderately tolerant
3 to 49	17 to 20	moderately intolerant
42 and below	16 and below	quite intolerant

If your score places you on the tolerant side of the continuum on both 2A and 2B, you should be well suited for diving into the more difficult aspects of your language. But don't let yourself become intellectually lazy. Make an effort to discern the complexities of the system, to figure out grammatical mysteries, to listen for correct forms, and to keep refining your own speaking skills.

If you scored on the intolerant side on both tests, then your challenge is to convince yourself that it's okay to be confused about how language works and at the same time to use it, even if you are not sure you are doing so correctly. In short, you've got to be willing to take some risks.

Your scores on 2A and 2B may have crossed over between tolerant and intolerant categories; that is, you were on the tolerant side on one test and intolerant on the other. Among those who took this test in its experimental form, a significant number fell into this cross-over category. If your scores were crossed, it may mean that you approach the specific task of learning a foreign language in a different way from other life situations. In such a case, use the strengths of one category to offset potential weaknesses in the other. Here are two rules of thumb:

1. If you were intolerant on 2A and tolerant on 2B, use the strength of your overall tendency to want to fit things together as a stimulus to decipher linguistic systems. Your naturally tolerant approach to the language itself will save you from feeling like you are drowning.
2. If you were tolerant on 2A and intolerant on 2B, use your overall tolerant style of thinking to convince yourself that the foreign language won't overwhelm you. Try to resist the temptation to fit all the linguistic bits and pieces into neat categories. Treat the foreign language as you do other things in your life.

For further consultation:

Chapelle, Carol, and Cheryl Roberts. "Ambiguity tolerance and field independence as predictors of proficiency in English as a second language." *Language Learning* 36 (1986): 27-45.

Norton, Robert W. "Measurement of ambiguity tolerance." *Journal of Personality Assessment* 39 (1975): 607-19.

Test 3: Left- and right-brain preference

In chapter 5, the concept of left- and right-brain functioning was described. Keep in mind that the left-brain/right-brain notion is really more a useful metaphor than a proven biological fact. The two categories are an enlightening way of describing some aspects of thinking styles and are especially illuminating in helping you understand how to tackle a foreign language.

A left-brain approach to language learning is analytical, systematic, and intellectual. You study the elements of language and search for systematic categories of sounds, words, grammar, and so forth. A right-brain approach is integrative, more socially and emotionally charged, flexible, spontaneous, and creative. You pay more attention to nonverbal communication—gestures, eye contact, body language—and to the whole message rather than to the separate components of language within a message.

Once again, both approaches are important. If the two hemispheres of the brain work together as a team, then you can optimize your chances for success.

On Test 3, a score of 60 is the midpoint. However, as the scoring chart below indicates, scores between 57 and 63 are a toss-up in terms of identifying your orientation.

Below 50	Quite left-brain oriented
50 - 56	Moderately left-brain oriented
57 - 63	No particular dominance on either side
64 - 70	Moderately right-brain oriented
Above 70	Quite right-brain oriented

If you were on the left-brain side of the continuum, your strength lies in your ability to figure out the rules and to apply them analytically. However, you could become too comfortable with this knowledge *about* the language. You may need to take more risks in unrehearsed conversations—just dive in and start talking even if you're not sure everything you say is grammatically correct.

If your score indicated a right-brain orientation, then you should take advantage of your ability to get the gist of a conversation in which you don't understand every word. Continue to trust your intuition as you extract meaning from language you can't fully analyze. You might need to push yourself to work a little harder on grammar and vocabulary than you are naturally inclined to. Some added attention to rules and structures could improve your accuracy.

If your score was in the middle category (57-63), it simply means you probably don't have a dominant preference for either type of processing. At times you may lean to the left, at others to the right. You can use your balance to your advantage by discerning the appropriate instances to apply one or the other orientation.

By now, you are probably quite capable of drawing further implications from left-brain/right-brain analysis (you may wish to review the section in chapter 5 that dealt with this topic). The important point is that your chances of success will be increased if you capitalize on the strengths of whatever your own orientation seems to be.

For further consultation:

Your Style of Learning and Thinking by E. Paul Torrance
Scholastic Testing Service, Inc.
P.O. Box 1056
Bensenville, IL 60106

Edwards, Betty. *Drawing on the Right Side of the Brain* (Los
Angeles: J. P. Tarcher/St. Martins, 1979).

Test 4: Visual and auditory learning

If you are learning a foreign language in the classroom, the teacher's overall method of handling the class can make a significant difference in your success. Your cognitive style preferences may or may not match the teacher's. A teacher with a strong left-brain orientation may be more difficult to understand if you happen to lean toward right-brain thinking. Or a particular method of instruction may or may not suit your style of learning. For example, if you prefer group work to individual work and the teacher relies on the latter, you could be at a slight disadvantage.

Yet another preference that often makes a significant difference in the classroom is visual versus auditory learning. Visual learners do better when something is presented through the printed word, drawings, blackboard illustrations, television, films, etc. Auditory learners do better with verbal presentations, audiotapes, and the like. People tend to develop a visual/auditory preference at a very young age and carry it through school and into adulthood.

In learning a foreign language, the extent to which your visual/auditory preference is emphasized can make a difference. When I was trying to learn Tagalog (spoken in the Philippines) in graduate school, the teacher insisted on a totally auditory approach. Her rationale was that if we saw the words written out, or if we wrote words down ourselves, it would interfere with our pronunciation. While she had a point, I was nevertheless frustrated. Writing things down helps to etch them in my memory. In the end I took written notes anyway, but somewhat surreptitiously.

Your score on Test 4 should be an indicator of your preference. If you do better with visual learning, then seize opportunities to write things down, draw pictures, and otherwise use your visual sense. If you feel strongly enough about it, talk to your teacher and ask him or her to consider using more visuals.

If you are an auditory learner, you will be better prepared to make the keen discrimination among sounds required to understand spoken language. The sound systems of language, like music, are complex and have many different elements: separate consonants and vowels, pauses between words and phrases, rhythm, tone, and emphasis, to name a few. If your classroom becomes too visually oriented, you may need to bring some auditory stimulation into your world. Listen to tapes, practice the language out loud to yourself, and encourage the teacher to talk more.

For further consultation:

"The Learning Style Inventory" by R. Dunn, K. Dunn, G.E.
Price
Price Systems
RR1 Box 214
Lawrence, KS 66044

Reid, Joy. "The learning style preferences of ESL students."
   TESOL Quarterly 21 (1987): 87-110.

Test 5: Language puzzle

This final little language puzzle is not so much a test as an exercise
in analysis. It simulates the kind of problem solving that you have to do
in many foreign language classes. The task in the puzzle is to figure out
inductively how the system works. Two aspects of the puzzle are
significant: (a) how many items you got right and (b) how long it took you
to work through the problems. Among the several possible profiles
below, find the one you fit into and read the interpretation.

Eleven or more correct answers in eight minutes or less. You
appear to have the kind of analytical problem-solving style that will lend
itself well to studying grammar and to figuring out how the system works
even when you don't know the rules. You are relatively fast and efficient
at this type of work. Use that efficiency to boost your confidence, but
make sure that you also spend plenty of time gaining conversational
proficiency as well.

Eleven or more answers correct in more than eight minutes. You
appear to have the kind of analytical problem-solving style that will lend
itself well to studying grammar and to figuring out how the system works
even when you don't know the rules. However, you may need more
time than others to effectively apply your analytical skills. Use your
ability to understand the system to boost your confidence, but make sure
that you allow yourself the time you need to learn the grammar.

Ten or fewer answers correct in eight minutes or less. The analytical problem solving involved in learning grammar may not be your

strong suit. You tend to work relatively rapidly but perhaps at the expense of accuracy. If you allow yourself more time to work on grammar, you may experience some improvement. Your strength probably lies in other aspects of foreign language learning, such as using the language meaningfully for personal interaction. Capitalize on that strength, but allow yourself the time you need to learn the grammar.

Ten or fewer answers correct in more than eight minutes. The analytical problem solving involved in learning grammar is probably not your strong suit. Understanding grammar may require a good deal of time and effort. Be prepared to put in that time and your efforts should be rewarded. Remember that your strength may lie in other aspects of foreign language learning, such as using the language meaningfully for personal interaction. Capitalize on that strength, but allow yourself the time you need to learn the grammar.

No matter which of the four categories you fall into, keep in mind the fact that grammatical analysis is just one aspect of language learning. There are many excellent language learners who are not good grammatical analyzers. You could be a right-brain learner who internalizes the language intuitively without analyzing it much. If you can make sense of the language intuitively, without conscious analysis of its grammar, you can still be an efficient language learner.

The problem is that many language classes—wisely or not—require a lot of grammar work. While you might want to argue that you can learn to speak the language without conscious focus on grammatical rules and exercises, your teacher, who holds the power of authority, may disagree. You may have to compromise: resolve to do what you can with the grammar, but prove to the teacher that even without it you can be a good communicator. A good teacher will ultimately measure your success according to how well you communicate.

For further consultation on the place of grammatical analysis in foreign language learning:

Krashen, Stephen. *The Input Hypothesis* (London: Longman, Inc., 1985).

Your "language quotient"

There is, of course, no such convention as a "language quotient," especially if, like IQ, it means adding up points on a test. The little tests in this book don't give you a language learning index or profile. Rather, they provide indicators of what a few of your style tendencies are at the present time. And even then, they need to be checked against what your intuition says about your preferred learning styles.

There are other ways to measure yourself. Go through this book and review the summaries at the end of each chapter. Evaluate how various factors apply specifically to you and your situation. Then, as you understand yourself better, you can develop a set of language learning strategies that will work successfully for you.

How to be a better language learner: A journal-writing approach

As you begin—or continue—your language study, you may wish to follow a systematic program to support and reinforce your classroom experience. The approach suggested here involves twelve steps which should be spread out evenly over the duration of your course. If you are not taking a formal course, you can modify the program to suit your own situation.

The key to success in following this twelve-step program is keeping a personal journal, or diary, in which you record feelings and thoughts as you proceed. Even if you have never kept a diary before, that's okay. It's not difficult to take a few minutes occasionally to write down your thoughts. Just find a sturdy notebook with plenty of blank pages in it and start writing. Your journal should be completely spontaneous. Any thought that comes into your head about yourself, your language class, your teacher, your classmates, or whatever, is worth jotting down.

Write something in your journal at least once a week. If you write less frequently, you may lose a train of thought or find it hard to gain perspective on your progress. Entries may be a sentence or two or several pages, depending on your mood at the time. Allow at least ten or fifteen minutes each time you write. Date your entries and every few weeks go back and read over what you wrote. In the twelve-step program outlined below, you will find topics suggested for each step. Don't feel bound by those topics however.

The payoff for keeping a personal journal will probably come sooner than you expect. Putting your thoughts and feelings in writing helps to clarify them and enables you to deal with them better. Difficult issues become less so. If nothing else, just using the journal to blow off steam can be helpful. By reflecting in writing on your experience, you will be better able to sort out which strategies are working for you and which are not.

A twelve-step program
for language learning

Step 1

If you have the option of choosing the kind of course you are going to take, then, before you even begin, carefully review the twelve criteria at the end of chapter 9 (pages 138-40). Write down the criteria that are the most important in your mind, and then try to find a course that meets as many of them as possible.

Before the first class session, review chapter 1 of this book. Then ask yourself why you want to learn this particular language. Write down your personal goals and state what you expect to actually do with the language in the future. Once you have stated your goals, keep a clear focus on them throughout the course. You may want to pin up a shortened version of these goals somewhere to help keep them in the forefront of your mind.

Step 2

As you start your course, what is your overall emotional state: overwhelmed? challenged? excited? Is the course too easy? a bunch of busywork? Do the rest of the students seem to know more than you? Are you especially delighted or frustrated by anything?

As you think about the goals you have formulated in step 1, consider the motivation behind those goals that will keep you moving ahead. Motivation is fed by certain drives or needs, as explained in chapter 6 (pages 86-88). Think about those needs, especially the need for exploration, stimulation, and ego-gratification. In your journal, describe the extent to which you feel driven by those three needs as they relate to your goals.

Step 3

How do you feel about your teacher? Have those feelings changed since the first day? Is the teacher supportive? Does the teacher reach out to the students, recognize differences (in terms of abilities and preferred strategies) among students? How would *you* teach this class?

How do you feel about your classmates? Do they seem to be better than you or not? Describe the general class spirit or mood. Is it helping or hindering your own process? If it is hindering you, is there anything you can do about changing that mood?

Step 4

Think about some of the principles of first-language acquisition (summarized at the end of chapter 2, page 21): using language for survival; taking language in subconsciously; being creative with language; listening a lot; connecting language with thinking. Do any of those apply to you? Could you benefit by putting any of them into practice at this point? How?

Do you feel any self-doubt right now? Does learning this language seem to be beyond your capacity? If so, think of all the things you do well, and list them in your journal. Now try to relate at least some of the items on your list to your language learning process, and in so doing tell yourself you can do it.

Step 5

Consider how children learn a second language (look at the end of chapter 3 for a reminder, pages 36-37) and ask yourself if you can borrow some of their secrets: not worrying about perfect pronunciation, not thinking too much about what you are doing; shedding your inhibitions; not letting your native language get in the way. How can you put those secrets to use? What kind of personal strategies might they lead you to adopt right now? Make a list in your journal.

Do you have any feelings of foreign language anxiety—fears of failure, of making mistakes, of looking stupid, or of being laughed at? Describe those fears, if any, and brainstorm specific things you can do to overcome them.

Step 6

Now that you are settling in to a routine (or are you?) in this class, do you feel better or worse than you did at the beginning? Do you still have the same feelings about the teacher and the method being used? Are you avoiding defensive learning? Are your classmates allies or competitors? (See chapter 4, page 44.)

Look again at the seven types of intelligence described by Gardner (chapter 4, pages 46-47). Where are your strengths? How can you capitalize on them? Have you tapped all of your intellectual resources? Look again at chapter 4 and assess the extent to which you are using as much of your brain as possible.

Step 7

How do your own general cognitive styles mesh with the flow of the class? Consider issues like ambiguity tolerance, reflectivity versus impulsivity, left- and right-brain orientation, and field sensitivity. Combine what you intuitively feel is your best cognitive style with what you learned about yourself from the tests taken in the Appendix, and then outline a program of strategies to work on. Do this exercise even if you only come up with a few hints like, "Don't be so sensitive about making mistakes," or "Stay cool and calm in the face of all this chaos."

You are well into the language learning process now. Encourage yourself to take the risk and plunge into conversations even if you don't feel sure of yourself. Try to seek out situations where you can converse.

Step 8

Have you tried any games to help you along? Pick some of the games listed toward the end of chapter 6 (pages 85-86) or invent your own and try them out. Then, in your journal, describe the extent to which they paid off for you.

Here is a game of sorts: In a bookstore, find a tourist phrase book for your target language. Look at some of the common phrases used for greetings and introductions, for ordering a meal in a restaurant, or for finding your way in a city. Practice some of the phrases with a partner. You might even attempt some role playing. Try to sound as much like a native speaker as possible. Don't get discouraged; it may take a while for the phrases to roll off your tongue. Record in your journal what you felt.

Step 9

Try to assess the extent to which you may be overmonitoring yourself at this point. Do you find yourself thinking about rules as you speak? Do you hesitate a lot because you are trying to get it just right (by the book)? If so, this mental zoom lens may be hindering you. Set your mind at a wider angle.

One way to use a linguistic wide-angle lens is to do as much listening as possible. Listen to tapes and watch videos and films in the target language. If possible, go to a movie with subtitles. That way you will understand what is happening but hear the language without analyzing it. Afterward, record your impressions of this experience in your journal.

Step 10

As you continue to make progress, do you feel any sense of language-ego involvement? Are you developing a second identity? Are you ready to join the language club? What are some of the rules for joining the particular language club you are trying to get into? (see chapter 7).

Write down your most candid feelings about the culture of the target language. Describe the people, their customs, and their attitudes. What can you learn from them?

Step 11

Think about the errors you habitually make, and write some of them down. Do they come from your native-language map—the system of English rules and patterns that you assume apply to the target language? What are you learning from your errors?

How is your pronunciation progressing now? Do you feel satisfied with it? If not, what difficulties are you having that you need to overcome? Make a list of those difficulties and work on them in the next few weeks, even if your language course is about to end.

Step 12

If you were lucky enough to be able to choose your language course, what do you think, now that it is over, about your choice? How many of the the twelve criteria for a good language course have been fulfilled? What sort of method did your teacher use? Do you think it was effective? Why? Are there any other methods (described in chapter 9) that you think might have improved the class? What should you look for in a follow-up course?

As you wrap up the course, do you feel you have made any breakthroughs—moments when you communicate without thinking about the language? Do you have a sense that at least some of your speech is automatic? Look back over your journal and assess your progress. Establish some goals for the next course, if you plan to take one, and consider working through these twelve steps again.

Break the language barrier!

The process of learning a foreign language is complex and intricate. But the rewards of reaching your goals are manifold. Through a healthy self-understanding, an awareness of the process you are going through, a confidence in your own abilities, and the determination to succeed, you can join the ranks of millions of people who have successfully broken the language barrier. Bon voyage!

Appendix

The reader is welcome to copy the tests in this Appendix for personal use.

Test 1

Directions: Circle either (a) or (b) for each item. Do not skip any items, even if you have a hard time placing yourself into one or the other category.

1. I usually like
   - (a) mixing with people.
   - (b) working alone.

2. I'm more inclined to be
   - (a) fairly reserved.
   - (b) pretty easy to approach.

3. I'm happiest when I'm
   - (a) alone.
   - (b) with other people.

4. At a party, I
   - (a) interact with many, including strangers.
   - (b) interact with a few—people that I know.

5. In my social contacts and groups, I usually
   - (a) get behind on the news.
   - (b) keep abreast of what's happening with others.

6. I can usually do things better by
    (a) figuring them out on my own.
    (b) talking with others about it.

7. My usual pattern when I'm with other people is
    (a) to be open, frank, and take risks.
    (b) to keep "myself to myself" and not be very open.

8. When I make friends, usually
    (a) someone else makes the first move.
    (b) I make the first move.

9. I would rather
    (a) be at home on my own.
    (b) go to a boring party.

10. Interaction with people I don't know
    (a) stimulates and energizes me.
    (b) taxes my reserves.

11. In a group of people I usually
    (a) wait to be approached.
    (b) initiate conversation.

12. When I'm by myself I usually feel a sense of
    (a) solitude.
    (b) loneliness.

13. In a classroom situation I prefer
    (a) group work, interaction with others.
    (b) individual work on my own.

14. When I get into a quarrel or argument, I prefer
    (a) being silent, hoping the issue will resolve itself or blow over.
    (b) to "have it out" and settle the issue right then and there.

15. When I try to put deep or complex thoughts into words, I usually
    (a) have quite a hard time.
    (b) do so fairly easily.

Scoring for Test 1

Mark an X corresponding to your choices in the grid below:

	a	b
1		
4		
7		
10		
13		

↑

	a	b
2		
5		
8		
11		
14		
+		

↑

	a	b
3		
6		
9		
12		
15		
+		= [ ]

↑

Add up the number of X's in *only* three of the columns, as indicated. Ignore all other X's. Total those three numbers to get a grand total, and put it in the large box at the right. This is your score for Test 1. For an interpretation of your score, read chapter 10, pages 143-45.

Test 2[52]

Directions: Circle the appropriate response for each item. "YES!" is equivalent to "strongly agree" and "NO!" to "strongly disagree." Mark your first impression and move quickly through all twenty-five items.

2A

1. Almost every problem has a solu-
   tion.   YES!   yes   ?   no   NO!

2. I like to fool around with new
   ideas, even if they are a total waste
   of time.   YES!   yes   ?   no   NO!

3. Nothing gets accomplished in this
   world unless you stick to some
   basic rules.   YES!   yes   ?   no   NO!

4. I believe that in the final analysis
   there is not a distinct difference
   between right and wrong.   YES!   yes   ?   no   NO!

5. Usually, the more clearly defined
   rules a society has, the better off it
   is.   YES!   yes   ?   no   NO!

6. Personally, I tend to think that
   there is a right way and a wrong
   way to do almost everything.   YES!   yes   ?   no   NO!

7. I prefer the certainty of always
   being in control of myself.   YES!   yes   ?   no   NO!

8. Once I start a task, I don't like to start another task until I finish the first one.   YES!   yes   ?   no   NO!

9. Before any important job, I must know how long it will take.   YES!   yes   ?   no   NO!

10. In a problem-solving group it is always best to systematically attack the problem.   YES!   yes   ?   no   NO!

11. A problem has little attraction for me if I don't think it has a solution.   YES!   yes   ?   no   NO!

12. I do not like getting started in group projects unless I feel assured that the project will be successful.   YES!   yes   ?   no   NO!

13. In a decision-making situation in which there is not enough information to process the problem, I feel very uncomfortable.   YES!   yes   ?   no   NO!

14. I don't like to work on a problem unless there is a possibility of coming out with a clear-cut and unambiguous answer.   YES!   yes   ?   no   NO!

15. Complex problems appeal to me only if I have a clear idea of the total scope of the problem.   YES!   yes   ?   no   NO!

16. A group meeting functions best with a definite agenda.   YES!   yes   ?   no   NO!

17. I am tolerant of ambiguous situations. YES! yes ? no NO!

18. The **best** part about working a jigsaw puzzle is putting in that last piece. YES! yes ? no NO!

For the last seven items think of the specific foreign language that you are now studying.

2B

19. I am bothered when I don't understand everything in the foreign language. YES! yes ? no NO!

20. I like to know specific rules for all aspects of grammar. YES! yes ? no NO!

21. I am satisfied with only a vague understanding of conversations in which I am a participant. YES! yes ? no NO!

22. Multiple or hidden meanings in the foreign language confuse me. YES! yes ? no NO!

23. I avoid reading material in the foreign language that I don't understand. YES! yes ? no NO!

24. I like my foreign language class to be structured so that I know just what is going to happen next. YES! yes ? no NO!

25. Starting to learn a new foreign language is scary. YES! yes ? no NO!

Scoring for Test 2

Score each item as follows: For most items the YES! scores 1 point and the NO! scores 5 points. A few items (*2, 4, 17, 21*) are reversed. Use the scoring table below for all items *except* 2, 4, 17, and 21:

Yes!	yes	?	no	NO!
1	2	3	4	5

Write your score for each of those items in the space to the right of Test 2. Now, score items 2, 4, 17, and 21 as follows:

Yes!	yes	?	no	NO!
5	4	3	2	1

Write those numbers to the right of those four items.

Now total items 1 through 18: _____(this is your score for Test 2A)

Then total items 19 through 25: _____(this is your score for Test 2B)

For interpretation of these scores, read chapter 10, pages 145-46.

Test 3[53]

Directions: Each item below has two contrasting statements. Between each statement is a scale of five points on which you are to indicate your perception of which statement best describes you. Boxes 1 and 5 indicate that a statement is very much like you; boxes 2 and 4 indicate that one statement is somewhat more like you than the other statement; box 3 indicates no particular leaning one way or the other. Example:

I prefer speaking to large audiences.	1 ☐	2 ☐	3 ☐	4 ☒	5 ☐	I prefer speaking in small-group situations.

Box number 4 has been checked to indicate a moderate preference for speaking in small-group situations.

	1	2	3	4	5	
1. I remember names.	☐	☐	☐	☐	☐	1. I remember faces.
2. I respond better to verbal instructions.	☐	☐	☐	☐	☐	2. I respond better to demonstrated, illustrated, symbolic instructions.
3. I am intuitive.	☐	☐	☐	☐	☐	3. I am intellectual.
4. I experiment randomly and with little restraint.	☐	☐	☐	☐	☐	4. I experiment systematically and with control.
5. I prefer solving a problem by breaking it down into parts, then approaching the problem sequentially, using logic.	☐	☐	☐	☐	☐	5. I prefer solving a problem by looking at the whole, the configurations, then approaching the problem through patterns, using hunches.

	1	2	3	4	5	
6. I make objective judgments, extrinsic to person.	☐	☐	☐	☐	☐	6. I make subjective judgments, intrinsic to person.
7. I am fluid and spontaneous.	☐	☐	☐	☐	☐	7. I am planned and structured.
8. I prefer certain, established information.	☐	☐	☐	☐	☐	8. I prefer elusive, uncertain information.
9. I am a synthesizing reader.	☐	☐	☐	☐	☐	9. I am an analytical reader.
10. I rely primarily on language in thinking and remembering.	☐	☐	☐	☐	☐	10. I rely primarily on images in thinking and remembering.
11. I prefer talking and writing.	☐	☐	☐	☐	☐	11. I prefer drawing and manipulating objects.
12. I get easily distracted trying to read a book in noisy or crowded places.	☐	☐	☐	☐	☐	12. I can easily concentrate on reading a book in noisy or crowded places.
13. I prefer work and/or studies that are open-ended.	☐	☐	☐	☐	☐	13. I prefer work and/ or studies that are carefully planned.
14. I prefer hierarchical (ranked) authority structures.	☐	☐	☐	☐	☐	14. I prefer collegial (participative) authority structures.

	1	2	3	4	5	
15. I control my feelings.	☐	☐	☐	☐	☐	15. I am free with my feelings.
16. I respond best to kinetic (movement, action) stimuli.	☐	☐	☐	☐	☐	16. I respond best to auditory and visual stimuli.
17. I am good at interpreting body language.	☐	☐	☐	☐	☐	17. I am good at paying attention to people's exact words.
18. I frequently use metaphors and analogies.	☐	☐	☐	☐	☐	18. I rarely use metaphors or analogies.
19. I favor logical problem solving.	☐	☐	☐	☐	☐	19. I favor intuitive problem solving.
20. I prefer multiple choice tests.	☐	☐	☐	☐	☐	20. I prefer open-ended questions.

Scoring for Test 3

Score each item as follows: Some of the items are scored according to the numbers at the top of each column of boxes, others are *reversed*. For the following items use the indicated numbers on the test page:

1	10
2	11
5	14
6	15
8	19
	20

□1 □2 □3 □4 □5

The rest of the items are *reversed* in their scoring. Score the following items using the numbers indicated at right.

3	9
4	12
7	13
	16
	17
	18

□5 □4 □3 □2 □1

Now total up all scores: _____
For interpretation of this score, read chapter 10, pages 147-48.

Test 4[54]

Directions: Circle either (a), (b), or (c).

1. I understand directions better when
    (a) the teacher tells them to me.
    (b) I read them.
    (c) no preference either way

2. I learn better when
    (a) I hear material from the teacher.
    (b) I read what the teacher writes on the chalkboard.
    (c) no preference

3. I understand explanations of concepts better when
    (a) I hear them.
    (b) I read them.
    (c) no preference

4. I remember words better when I
    (a) hear them spoken out loud.
    (b) see them in writing.
    (c) no preference

5. I prefer
    (a) listening to lectures.
    (b) reading a textbook.
    (c) no preference

6. I prefer
    (a) to hear a story.
    (b) to read a story.
    (c) no preference

7. I remember
    (a) sounds better.
    (b) pictures better.
    (c) no preference

Scoring for Test 4

Number of (a) answers: _____ (Auditory)

Number of (b) answers: _____ (Visual)

[don't count (c) answers]

If (a) is larger, you prefer *auditory* learning.

If (b) is larger, you prefer *visual* learning.

For an interpretation of your score, read chapter 10, pages 148-49.

Test 5[55]

Directions: The list below contains words from another language with its English equivalents.

munto	a person
chibo	a dog
munto chibulu vova	A person hears a dog.

Using the information above, figure out how the following statement should be expressed in this language. Do this without writing on paper.

A dog hears a person.

Do *not* read ahead until you have decided on an answer.

The answer to the problem is *chibo muntulu vova*. Notice that the word in the sentence that receives the action (*munto*) is changed: the last vowel becomes *u* and a *lu* is added. If you didn't answer the problem correctly, look at it again and you should now understand it.

There are sixteen similar problems on the next three pages.

Before you turn the page...

Look at your watch or a clock, and write the exact time (to the minute) that you start the problems on the next page. (You can set a stopwatch if you have one.) Then, as soon as you finish the sixteen problems, look at the time (or stop your stopwatch) and calculate the number of minutes you took to complete the test.

Now turn to the next page...

Read the problems carefully and indicate your answer by circling one of the four choices for each problem.

munto	a person
chibo	a dog
munto chibulu vova	A person hears a dog.
munto chibulu vovele	A person heard a dog.
wawa	sees

Using the above list, figure out how to say each of the sentences below. Circle the option you think is correct.

1. A person sees a dog.
    a. chibo muntulu wawa
    b. munto chibulu wawa
    c. munto wawa chibulu
    d. chibo wawa muntulu

2. A dog sees a person.
    a. chibo muntulu wawa
    b. munto chibulu wawa
    c. munto wawa chibulu
    d. chibo wawa muntulu

3. A person saw a dog.
    a. chibo muntulu wawele
    b. munto chibo wawele
    c. munto wawele chibulu
    d. munto chibulu wawele

4. A dog saw a person.
    a. chibo muntulu wawele
    b. chibo munto wawele
    c. chibo wawele muntulu
    d. munto chibulu wawele

Now continue the test, using the list below, which contains the words in the original list above, and some additional ones.

---

munto	a person
chibo	a dog
munto chibulu vova	A person hears a dog.
munto chibulu vovele	A person heard a dog.
wawa	sees
be	we
ge	you
chibulu bevova	We hear a dog.
gulu bevova	We hear you.
gulu kibevova	We don't hear you.

---

5. We see a dog.
   a. bewawa chibulu
   b. chibulu bewawele
   c. chibulu bewawa
   d. chibulu bevovele

6. We saw a dog.
   a. bewawa chibulu
   b. chibulu bewawele
   c. chibulu bewawa
   d. chibulu bevovele

7. We see you.
   a. gulu bewawa
   b. bulu gewawele
   c. gulu bevova
   d. bulu gewawa

8. You see us.
   a. gulu bewawa
   b. bulu gewawele
   c. gulu bevova
   d. bulu gewawa

9. We heard you.
   a. muntulu gevova
   b. gulu bevovele
   c. muntulu gevovele
   d. gulu bevova

10. You heard a person.
   a. muntulu gevova
   b. gulu bevovele
   c. muntulu gevovele
   d. gulu bevova

munto	a person
chibo	a dog
munto chibulu vova	A person hears a dog.
munto chibulu vovele	A person heard a dog.
wawa	sees
be	we
ge	you
chibulu bevova	We hear a dog.
gulu bevova	We hear you.
gulu kibevova	We don't hear you.

11. A dog saw us.
    a. chibulu bewawa
    b. chibulu bewawele
    c. chibo bulu wawele
    d. chibo bulu kiwawele

12. A dog didn't see us.
    a. chibulu bewawa
    b. chibulu bewawele
    c. chibo bulu wawele
    d. chibo bulu kiwawele

13. You don't hear a dog.
    a. chibulu kigewawele
    b. chibulu kigevova
    c. chibulu kibevova
    d. chibulu kigewawa

14. You didn't see a dog.
    a. chibulu kigewawele
    b. chibulu kigevova
    c. chibulu kibevova
    d. chibulu kigewawa

15. A person heard you.
    a. munto gulu vovele
    b. munto vovele ge
    c. munto gulu wawele
    d. gulu munto wawele

16. A person saw you.
    a. munto gulu vovele
    b. gulu munto vovele
    c. munto gulu wawele
    d. ge munto wawele

Scoring for Test 5

Check your watch right away and calculate the number of minutes you took to complete the test. Put that number in the second blank below. Now, look at the answers below and indicate your correct answers. Total up the number of correct answers and put the number in the first blank.

1.	b	9.	b
2.	a	10.	c
3.	d	11.	c
4.	a	12.	d
5.	c	13.	b
6.	b	14.	a
7.	a	15.	a
8.	d	16.	c

Total number correct: _____

Number of minutes to complete the test: _____

For an interpretation of your score, see chapter 10 , pages 150-51.

EndNOTES

Chapter 1.   CAN I LEARN A FOREIGN LANGUAGE?

1.   J. William Fulbright, "We're tongue-tied," *Newsweek*, 30 July 1979, 15.
2.   Paul Simon, *The Tongue-Tied American: Confronting the Foreign Language Crisis* (New York: The Continuum Publishing Corp., 1980), 5.
3.   *Strength through Wisdom: A Critique of U.S. Capability* (A report to the president from the President's Commission on Foreign Language and International Studies, November 1979).
4.   These statistics are taken from circulars distributed by the Joint National Committee for Languages, Washington, D.C., 1986-1988. See also Lindsey Gruson, "U.S. working to close foreign language gap," *New York Times*, 2 December 1986.

Chapter 2.   HOW BABIES LEARN TO TALK

5.   Frank Smith, "The promise and threat of microcomputers for language learners", in *On TESOL '83: The Question of Control*, edited by Jean Handscombe, Richard Orem, and Barry Taylor (Washington, DC: Teachers of English to Speakers of Other Languages, 1983), 2.
6.   Noam Chomsky, *Aspects of the Theory of Syntax* (Cambridge, MA: MIT Press, 1965).
7.   Derek Bickerton, *Roots of Language* (Ann Arbor, MI: Karoma Publishers, 1981).

8.   Ambrose Bierce, *The Devil's Dictionary* (New York: Doubleday Inc., 1967).
9.   Abraham Maslow, *Motivation and Personality*, 2nd ed. (New York: Harper and Row, 1970).
10.   St. Augustine, *Confessions*, translated by Edward Pusey (Oxford: J. C. Parker Company, 1838).
11.   Roger Brown and Ursula Bellugi, "Three processes in the child's acquisition of syntax," *Harvard Educational Review* 34 (1966): 134.
12.   Jean Berko, "The child's learning of English morphology," *Word* 14 (1958).
13.   Frank Smith and George A. Miller, eds., *The Genesis of Language* (Cambridge, MA: MIT Press, 1966), 69.
14.   Lewis Carroll, *Through the Looking Glass* (Boston: Lee and Shepard, 1872).
15.   David McNeill, "Developmental psycholinguistics," in *Verbal Behavior and General Behavior Theory*, edited by T. R. Dixon and D. L. Horton (Englewood Cliffs, NJ: Prentice-Hall, Inc., 1968).
16.   Herbert H. Clark and Eve Clark, *Psychology and Language: An Introduction to Psycholinguistics*, (New York: Harcourt Brace Jovanovich, Inc., 1977).

Chapter 3.   WHAT CHILDREN CAN TEACH US

17.   Quoted by H. H. Stern, *Perspectives on Second Language Teaching* (Toronto: Ontario Institute for Studies in Education, 1970), 58.
18.   Mark Twain, *The Innocents Abroad*, vol. I (New York: Harper and Brothers, 1869), 111.
19.   For a summary of research on lateralization, see H. Douglas Brown, *Principles of Language Learning and Teaching*, 2nd ed. (Englewood Cliffs, NJ: Prentice-Hall, Inc., 1987).
20.   Alexander Guiora et al., "The effects of experimentally induced changes in ego states on pronunciation ability in a second language: An exploratory study," *Comprehensive Psychiatry* 13 (1972).

Chapter 4.   USING YOUR BRAIN POWER

21.   B. F. Skinner, *Behavior of Organisms: An Experimental Analysis* (New York: Appleton-Century-Crofts, 1938).
22.   Howard Gardner, *Frames of Mind: The Theory of Multiple Intelligences* (New York: Basic Books, 1983).
23.   Robert J. Sternberg, *Beyond IQ: A Triarchic Theory of Human Intelligence* (New York: Cambridge University Press, 1985). For an update on Sternberg's theory of intelligence, see also Robert J. Sternberg, *The Triarchic Mind: A New Theory of Intelligence* (New York: Viking Penguin, Inc., 1988).
24.   Sheila Ostrander and Lynn Schroeder, *Superlearning* (New York: Dell Publishing Company, 1979), 13.
25.   Ibid.

26.   Georgi Lozanov, *Suggestology and Outlines of Suggestopedy* (New York: Gordon and Breach Science Publishers, 1979).

27.   Frank Smith, *Comprehension and Learning: A Conceptual Framework for Teachers* (New York: Holt, Rinehart & Winston, 1975), 162.

28.   Robert W. Blair, "Easification," in *Innovative Approaches to Language Teaching*, edited by Robert W. Blair (Rowley, MA: Newbury House Publishers, 1982), 221.

Chapter 5.   STRATEGIES FOR SUCCESS

29.   E. Paul Torrance, *Your Style of Learning and Thinking* (Bensenville, IL: Scholastic Testing Service, Inc., 1987).

30.   Betty Edwards, *Drawing on the Right Side of the Brain* (Los Angeles: J. P. Tarcher/St. Martins, 1979).

31.   Tadanobu Tsunoda, *The Japanese Brain* (Tokyo: Daishukan Shoten, 1978). [in Japanese]

32.   For a summary, consult Karl C. Diller, ed., *Individual Differences and Universals in Language Learning Aptitude* (Rowley, MA: Newbury House Publishers, 1981).

33.   Leonard Bernstein, "Visit as a friend—learn their language before you go," *House Beautiful* 116 (1974): 123-24.

Chapter 6.   I'M OK—I CAN DO IT!

34.   Thomas A. Harris, *I'm OK—You're OK* (New York: Avon Books, 1967).

35.   Wayne W. Dyer, *Pulling Your Own Strings* (New York: Avon Books, 1978).

36.   Barbara Utley, "Doing math is an emotional experience," *Ann Arbor News*, 9 November 1978.

37.   Eric Berne, *Games People Play* (New York: Grove Press, Inc., 1964), 1.

38.   Maslow, *Motivation and Personality*.

Chapter 7.   JOINING THE LANGUAGE CLUB

39.   Rick Horowitz, "Politics to the max," *San Francisco Chronicle*, December 1986.

40.   Frank Smith, "Joining the spoken language club" (Lecture delivered at San Francisco State University, 3 November 1984).

41.   Ibid.

42.   François Lierres, "How to get along with Americans," *Le Point*, 1975.

43.   Frank Vizitelly, ed., *The New Standard Encyclopedia* (New York: Funk & Wagnalls, 1940).

44.   Margaret Mead, "Discussion," in *Approaches to Semiotics*, edited by Thomas A. Sebeok, Alfred S. Hayes, and Mary Catherine Bateson (The Hague: Mouton Publishers, 1964), 189.

45.   Quoted by David Bycina, "Haragei," *JALT Newsletter* 3 (1979): 17.

Chapter 8.   MAKING YOUR MISTAKES WORK FOR YOU

46. Nelson Brooks, *Teacher's Manual* (New York: Modern Language Materials Development Center, 1961), 47.
47. The technical research jargon does not use these two terms in this way; rather, what I call "goofs" here are called "mistakes," and what I call "mistakes" here are called "errors." See H. Douglas Brown, *Principles of Language Learning and Teaching.*
48. Neddy A. Vigil and John W. Oller, "Rule fossilization: A tentative model," *Language Learning* 26 (1976): 281-95.

Chapter 9.   CHOOSING YOUR CLASSROOM METHOD

49. Terry Kirkpatrick, "Animated teacher stirs students," *Ann Arbor News*, 16 April 1978, F-8.
50. François Gouin, *L'art d'enseigner et d'étudier les langues* (Paris: Librairie Fischbacher, 1880).

Chapter 10.   CREATING YOUR OWN PATHWAY

51. *The Myers-Briggs Type Indicator* (Palo Alto, CA: Consulting Psychologists Press, Inc. 1987). *Eysenck Personality Inventory* (San Diego, CA: Educational and Industrial Testing Service, 1963).

Appendix

52. Items 1 through 18 of this test are taken from Robert W. Norton's "Measurement of Ambiguity Tolerance," *Journal of Personality Assessment* 39 (1975): 616-18.
53. Adapted from E. Paul Torrance's *Your Style of Learning and Thinking.*
54. This test is based on Joy Reid's "The learning style preferences of ESL students," *TESOL Quarterly* 21 (1987): 87-110.
55. Adapted from the Pimsleur Language Aptitude Battery (The Psychological Corporation, 1966).

Index